Duty (

By
Thomas Waugh

First published in 2023 by Sharpe Books.

DUTY CALLS

"A deception that elevates us is dearer than a host of low truths."
Alexander Pushkin.

"One doesn't know what one doesn't know."
Ivan Turgenev.

"So? If I die, then I die! The loss to the world won't be great."
Mikhail Lermontov.

1.

London. 2021.
The Skylon Restaurant.

Daniel Ambler yawned, not quite knowing if he was doing so out of tiredness or boredom. The author at least displayed the courtesy of waiting until his lunch companion, Simon Birch, averted his gaze. Ambler may have been indifferent towards most things in the world, but he still believed in the virtue of politeness. "Good manners cost nothing, but are priceless," his late father had said to him on more than one occasion.

Birch turned his attention back to his old university friend, having watched the shapely waitress walk away. The MI6 officer and spy novelist resumed their conversation.

"As well as your latest novel, I also read your recent piece in *The Sunday Telegraph*. You still seem to be fighting the good fight against the old - and new - Marxists. Or university lecturers and their gullible students, as we call them nowadays. Even Lenin called them "useful idiots". Unfortunately, these odious graduates are gaining employment at other institutions. Most of them are calling for a revolution. What they really need are a nice girlfriend, a good steak and a higher disposable income. They are useless idiots, in my book. But what was it that you wrote? The phrase "Marxist hypocrisy" may be seen as a tautology and the idea of "Marxist thought" is an oxymoron," Birch remarked, smiling and twiddling the stem of his wine glass. He then ran his palm along his already slicked-back hair a couple of times. His voice spoke of a man who had attended *Harrow* and *Magdalen College* - and was a member of the *Athenaeum* and *Carlton* clubs. It spoke of a husband whose wife did not need to work and whose children attended *Harrow* too.

"Communism may not necessarily be flawed, and it shouldn't necessarily descend into tyranny and statism. It just always does. Marx should not be considered a prophet, *Das Capital* is not the Bible and socialism isn't the promised land. It's perhaps unsurprising how so many evangelical atheists turn to political religions. To quote G. K. Chesterton: "When a man stops believing in God, he doesn't believe in nothing, he believes in anything." Climate change seems to be a new source of religion now. The first sin against climate change is the denial of climate change. The end of the world has always been big box office for demagogues. It seems that the rich can afford remittances in the form of carbon offsetting. I think it's quite sweet that there are people out there determined to save a planet, whose inhabitants they appear to despise. I might have some compassion for some of these ill-dressed zealots, if I didn't have so much contempt for them. They talk of social justice, mainly on *TikTok* of all places. Behind a mask of self-righteousness lies an all too human face. A foolish, vindictive face. Apparently, I was recently no-platformed by a university. I was booked to give a guest lecture. A "Friends of Palestine" student group protested, arguing I was Jewish and a friend of Israel. Which surprised me a little, I must say. I may sometimes consider myself a lapsed Catholic, but surely I'm not that lapsed as to have converted to Judaism? Ironically, they deemed I was Jewish from my Christian name. I would have been creating an unsafe space at the institution. I wouldn't put too much stock in the article, however. It was a trifling thing, which took a trifling amount of time. When the newspapers start paying a pound a word again, I might compose something more meaningful. It's unlikely though," Ambler replied, taking another sip (or a measure larger than a sip) of his more than tolerable Pomerol.

"You were always too hard on yourself, even back in college. You were your worst or best critic. Several of my colleagues are fans of your novels, including my boss."

"Let us hope that we do not need to worry about how reliable his judgement is on more important matters."

"You have a tendency to joke about your work and profession too. I warrant that your books have helped change the lives of some people."

Ambler smiled. Nearly toothily. Almost laughing.

"Authors do not change the world. Most of them are incapable of even changing their socks each day."

"You have elevated glibness to a religion, Daniel."

"There are worse things that one can have faith in. Glibness will never be a vengeful deity. At worst it'll be wistful. But to be serious rather than glib for the moment, we have now drunk our first bottle. Your training dictates that it's time you made your play, no? I haven't seen you in over six months, Simon. Out of the blue, you have invited me for lunch. And offer to pay for it, to boot. The Skylon is the limit it seems. You have even read my last book - or at least read the blurb and one or two reviews. Call me cynical, but I dare say I am here for an ulterior motive. You may work for MI6, but I can give you special dispensation to be honest for once. It's fine if you want to ask for use of my flat in Kensington again, should you wish to arrange another assignation."

"If only it were that, for various reasons," Birch said, moving his chair a little closer to the table, lowering his voice and knitting his brow. "I will be candid. This lunch concerns business rather than pleasure," he added, intriguingly or ominously.

The intelligence officer suddenly stopped talking, however, as the young, French waitress returned with their second bottle of wine. Birch offered the blonde would-be actress a suggestive look. Much to his chagrin, the waitress ignored him and flashed a smile at his effortlessly handsome friend (which Ambler returned

3

with a polite rather than amorous expression). Perhaps she would be impressed if he told her that he worked for MI6 - "a clown at the circus," as Ambler had once joked in a novel. His profession had impressed his wife, Sandra. It got her into bed, a decade ago. It had also got her to walk down the aisle, unfortunately. Birch's marriage was as happy as the next man's, if the next man was unhappily married. The waitress took her leave, after the oleaginous customer uttered a few complimentary words in her native language. She smiled politely, or awkwardly.

Birch was clean-shaven. His skin was not quite as smooth as the silk tie he wore, but that was the aim. His suit was expensive, but not made to measure. His father had worked for the Foreign Office, then MI6, and possessed a pension that even a veteran BBC commissioning editor would envy. What with attending Harrow and Oxford - and being his father's son - Birch easily secured a job at MI6. He was the right sort. The best sort. He looked like a slightly overweight Damian Lewis, with wine-stained lips and off-white teeth. Birch gave himself a suitable air of superiority. Arrogance supplanted confidence a long time ago. He had been a member of *The Bullingdon Club*, but a forgettable one. One nobody thought to take a photograph of. Birch believed that most women he encountered found him attractive, but he was far from the only would-be alpha male guilty of that particular conceit. For the past seven years he had worked on the Russia desk. Frustratingly, the budgets and resources had been weighted towards the Middle East during his time at the River House. But thankfully his servile masters were beginning to realise that the old enemy was also the current enemy. Finally, Birch was about to make a difference and a name for himself. He just needed Ambler to want to make a difference and a name for himself too.

Ambler was dressed in a pale blue shirt. Sans tie. The top button was undone. He had never undone a second, throughout his entire forty years plus on the planet. He wore an off-white linen jacket with off-white linen trousers, but from two different suits. Both purchased from *Brooks Brothers*. Ambler looked good for his age, despite rather than because of the drink. He certainly looked better than he often felt. His expression could be calm, contented, stoical or bored - depending on the circumstances, and how much drink he consumed. If life was a joke, he was able to laugh along with it (most of the time). Ambler was not beyond appearing weary and weathered, but he did so in private or when he thought no one else was watching. During his years at university and just afterwards he had been described as "Byronic-looking". Recently he had been called "Jewish-looking". Ambler had shrugged his shoulders, literally and figuratively, at both descriptions. His black hair, peppered with a few grey hairs, was cropped short. "Short hair is one less thing to worry about, so I can spend more time with my depression," he had half-joked in a profile piece last month.

After gaining a First at Oxford in European Literature and Russian Studies, Ambler worked in a bookshop in Hammersmith while he completed writing a biography of the Russian poet and novelist Mikhail Lermontov - *Lermontov: A Hero For All Time*. The book more than washed its face - and even garnered praise in Russia. Ambler followed up his debut with a short biography of Chekhov. He inserted himself into the London literary scene, attending parties and giving talks. He was photographed leaving restaurants with (RADA trained) actresses and (non-glamour) models. He started to review for the newspapers and then wrote comment pieces - making friends and enemies alike. His next book was the acclaimed historical novel, *Too Soon Gone*, concentrating on the last days of Alexander Pushkin. Whenever anyone praised Ambler, however, he thanked them and urged them to read T. J. Binyon's biography of his hero. It was "a much better book". The novel made *The Sunday Times* bestseller list and was optioned to be turned into a film (which was still in development, of course). For the past ten years, though, Ambler had been on a treadmill writing spy novels. He had been compared favourably to le Carré, Alan Furst and Charles Cumming. Three years ago, Birch had contacted his old friend and called him in to the River House to consult on an operation to reach out to Sergei Sharikov - a senior Russian history professor with insider knowledge of the Kremlin, who Ambler had become friends with. Someone had photographed the novelist coming out of the famed building, in the snow, and sold the picture to *The Daily Mail*. "*The Spy Who Came Out Into The Cold*" ran the headline. Ambler strenuously denied being an operative for MI6. But a spy would deny being a spy, more than one commentator argued. Denial somehow meant confirmation, whilst confirmation would not mean denial. As much as Ambler felt uncomfortable about the episode, his agent and publisher duly rubbed their hands together and fed the rumour-mill. At one point, due to press harassment, Ambler had to employ a driver, who doubled up as a close protection officer. A year later the Head of MI6, Ruth Starr, was asked if Daniel Ambler had ever been in the pay of the intelligence community. Due to being paid a small fee for his consultancy work with Birch, she was obliged to answer yes (denial probably would have meant confirmation again, and Starr was mindful of being caught in a lie). Ironically, Ambler was nearly in the pay of Starr six months later. She left her post and was offered a book deal to write spy novels. It transpired that she could barely string a sentence together and Ambler was approached to ghost write the books. At the time he needed to work on his marriage, rather than someone else's novels, so Ambler turned the lucrative contract down. But his career was an enviable one. Sales (of new and backlist titles) were good. Life was good (aside from a failed marriage, shards of Catholic guilt and back pain from a car accident a few months ago). Ambler just felt that he was somehow waiting for something to happen in his life. He just didn't know what that "something" could or should be.

"Have you ever heard the name Viktor Rybin?"

Ambler paused. He had heard of plenty of names, many of them Russian. But a picture of a humourless man with dark, deep-set eyes came into his head. Iron-grey hair and a beak of a nose. He was a cross between an accountant and undertaker. Ambler mined what he could from his memory (which he had to confess was growing a little duller with age, and booze). Rybin was a lieutenant in Vladimir Putin's inner circle. "He sits at the right-hand of God, like Michael - and is willing to smite like the archangel too," a journalist had once commented to him. Rybin had acted as a diplomat and speechwriter for the Russian president, but he had also served as a henchman. Allegedly, of course. Viktor Rybin had recently been photographed with a rapacious former British prime minister, presenting a grant to Cambridge University. The choleric statesman appeared like he was in actual physical discomfort, having to smile for the cameras. The former prime minister grinned like an idiot, however, perhaps recalling the day rate that he was charging the Russians or university. Or both.

"The name seems vaguely familiar," Ambler said, his expression the equivalent of a shrug. "It is best to never put all your cards on the table," the protagonist of one of the novelist's spy thrillers had once remarked. Ignorance is bliss. Feigning ignorance can have its benefits too.

"Let me give you some immediate context. If we consider Putin to be Al Capone, Viktor Rybin is his Frank Nitti. Rybin first served under Putin in the KGB, when the president was just a lowly intelligence officer in Hamburg. He next pops up on our radar as an "administrative assistant" to Putin, during his time as Deputy Mayor of St Petersburg. Rybin called himself a bureaucrat, but he has more blood on his hands than ink. Intelligence suggests that Rybin operated as the principal go-between when Putin forged links with the Tambov gang. Allegedly, of course. Our codename for Rybin is "Rasputin". He has the ear of Putin - and we believe that senior Russian officials often whisper certain names into their comrade's ear, for him to then disappear. His name was kept out of the official reports, but Rybin was in the UK during the Salisbury poisonings. We believe he was the author behind certain threatening letters that the likes of Berezovsky and Litvinenko received. He has never been married, unless you count being married to one's job. He has risen through the ranks through his efficiency and ruthlessness, as opposed to his charm and people skills. He is also a teetotaller -

and we both know how one can never entirely trust a man you can't get drunk with. Like his employer, Rybin is an idealogue. A zealot. Once a KGB agent, always a KGB agent. He believes in the greater Russian Empire, acts more paranoid than a cocaine addict and has an appetite for underage prostitutes, boys and girls. He labels us imperialists and capitalists in the propaganda he pens, although that does not prevent him from heavily investing in the London property market. Viktor Rybin has made a killing, in more ways than one. Obviously, Putin will live forever, like Big Brother, but should he have a list of possible successors then Rybin will be closer to the top than bottom. Rybin is a man who we can call, with not a little understatement, thoroughly unpleasant. He is a man who knows where the bodies are buried, because he put them there himself. Suffice to say, Rybin is a person of interest to us."

Birch heard the clicking of heels upon the polished wooden floor and ceased talking. The waitress returned with their starters. Birch thanked her in a brief, perfunctory manner this time. She was now an unwelcome distraction, disturbing his train of thought and pitch. He also caught a smell of her perfume and considered it cheap. The clicking of heels retreated once more.

"And why should Rybin be of interest to me? Is he releasing a novel that you would like me to write a scathing review of?" Ambler said, not knowing how genuinely nonchalant he was or how much he was pretending.

"You have become a victim of your own success, Daniel. Notoriety can be a blessing as well as a curse, and so on. Our desk has recently been contacted, with an offer of treasure. Which could prove genuine gold dust, rather than mere sand and glitter. You are friends with one Yevgeny Vetrov?"

Ambler pictured the Russian's porcine features, combover, claret-stained lips, flabby liver-spotted hands and wiry beard, often littered with crumbs of food. He heard the man's deep snort of a laugh. The writer originally met Vetrov at the Moscow launch party for the Russian edition of *Too Soon Gone*. The portly oligarch was a Pushkin obsessive. He had bid a substantial sum to pay for the alleged bullet which had killed the poet in his fateful duel with the French nobleman George D'Anthès. Vetrov also offered to pay Ambler two thousand dollars on the night of their initial meeting, so as to have lunch with him the following day. Much to the irritation of the author's literary agent, Ambler accepted the invitation but declined any payment. Vetrov was overweight and over-opinionated - but had diligently read his novel. A writer can excuse a multitude of sins in a soul, if they have read (or even just purchased) their book. The lunch was long and lavish. The two men remained in contact over the years. Vetrov opened some doors and introduced Ambler to some useful contacts when he came to write his spy novels. Such was Vetrov's eagerness to read Ambler's first cold war thriller that he employed an interpreter to read the English version to him in Russian on its release. The former steel magnate fell foul of Putin's regime when he became an ally of Boris Berezovsky. Vetrov now resided in Cuba. Every year Vetrov would write to Ambler, after reading his latest novel, and request that he sign and dedicate a dozen copies to his friends. The novelist was all too aware of some of the Russian's crimes and misdemeanours, but as all authors know - a sale is a sale.

"I wouldn't necessarily say we are friends, but we know each other," Ambler stated, as if he were answering a question in a deposition, after advice from his legal counsel. His eyes narrowed and features tightened in an expression that could no longer be deemed nonchalant.

"Two days ago, Vetrov, through a trusted intermediary, contacted my boss. He has offered us, what he calls, "compromising material" on Viktor Rybin. We have found no reason to doubt the veracity of his offer. Vetrov has motive. The two men even despised each other when they were batting for the same team. Rybin took an active part in denuding the oligarch of a vast swathe of his fortune, before sending him into exile. Vetrov would have had the opportunity to gather intelligence on his enemy too, during their past dealings. Blackmail material is both a source of investment and insurance in Putin's Russia. As to why he is now making the treasure available, we have confirmed that Vetrov has terminal pancreatic cancer. It seems that he wants to die, knowing that he will help vanquish his enemy. Not even the most diligent of Russian wet squads will be able to get to their target in the afterlife. We already requested that it would be preferable to send an agent to collect any material. Despite certain reports in the newspapers to the contrary, you are not an MI6 operative. But Vetrov's emissary was adamant. He will only hand the material over to you - and you alone - in person. The oligarch wants to play the diva one last time, it seems. Perhaps he wants to repent and offer you his last confession, although if he wants to confess his entire sins then you may be by his bedside for some days. Vetrov likes and trusts you. You have a history together. You may not call him a friend, but he calls you one. As much as he yearns to leave his mark on the world, or ruin Rybin, we do not want to try and call his bluff and insist on alternative arrangements. It's important that we keep our fish on the line. If the intelligence we receive can somehow remove Rybin from the board, then the planet will be a nicer and safer place. An author can sometimes change the world for the better. I know that it could require you to make a leap of faith, to believe that all will be well Daniel, but it is a leap worth taking," Birch argued, hoping to hook the fish of his friend. He had assured his boss, Boyd Hamilton, that he would be able to recruit the civilian and get the job done. Bring back the treasure. Birch asserted that he believed in the value of the operation - but subtly or otherwise argued that, if successful, he would merit a promotion.

Ambler paused once more. He took another non-sip of wine. He no longer felt like eating, however. He felt sick to his stomach and imagined that anything he now ate might turn into dead sea fruit. The author couldn't remember the last time that he had been taken back or lost for words. He soon regained his composure and wryness, though. Perhaps glibness was indeed his north star.

"The scenario seems so absurd, that you must be being serious. I feel like I am being written into the plot of one of my novels - and not one of my better ones either. I am also regretting having written such a barbed article against communism. Cuba is already fallow ground, in terms of book sales. I may not be welcomed with open arms in Havana. Communists are not known for being forgiving. But I am not sure why I should be even entertaining the idea. I suspect that the world will be as equally an unpleasant place, with or without Viktor Rybin's influence upon it. You say that I should make a leap of faith. I have faith in my scepticism - and at present a choir of angels are telling me to doubt that all will be well. Have you not read my books? Spy novels seldom contain happy endings."

"The experience could provide you with material for your next bestseller," Birch suggested, before finishing off his scallops and carefully dabbing the corner of his mouth with a napkin.

"It'll be somewhat difficult to write the next novel with seven grammes of lead lodged in my skull," Ambler replied, not being completely droll.

"The operation will be a secure one. Your safety will be our highest priority. We have been promised that the material he has in his possession cannot be traced back to Vetrov, therefore it will be nigh on impossible to be subsequently traced back to you," Birch assured his old friend, not being entirely truthful.

"How many people already know about this proposal?" Ambler asked, fearing that he may already have a target on his back. There should be no gradations of "impossible". Was his steak about to be served with a garnish of Polonium 210?

"Not many. The fewer the better, is best. My boss has kept things need to know. A couple of our analysts have been informed, as they have needed to assess the authenticity of Vetrov's offer. We run a tight ship. It is also in Vetrov's interests to be discreet. Think of it as taking a short trip to research a novel - and visit a contact there. You will not even have to bring the file back with you. We can arrange for a handoff with our man in Havana, so to speak. You can do this, Daniel. I remember drinking with you, late into the night, at college. You said that you wanted to do some good in the world. You will never get a better opportunity than this. Duty is calling," Birch said, whilst scrutinising his friend - as if he were a card player looking for tells in his opponent. "Convince Ambler that he will be the hero in his own story," Birch's boss had advised, smiling thinly.

"I was in my early twenties then. A damned fool. I am firmly a cynic now, as opposed to an idealist. If duty is calling, I'd rather not pick-up. Or I will just pretend it's a poor signal. Duty may be calling, but I fear I am unable to hear it over my indifference. I have seen enough of the world to know that it doesn't deserve to be saved."

A pregnant, or stillborn, pause briefly hung in the air.

"Are you finished?" the sweet-natured waitress asked the eerily silent diners.

"Yes," Ambler answered, a little curtly as if Birch had asked the question, despite half his starter remaining on his plate. He was tempted to throw his napkin down on the table and tell Birch that the entire lunch was over. Perhaps he didn't do so from a sense of etiquette and politeness. Or his stomach still hankered after the steak he ordered. Or maybe his mind still wasn't wholly made up.

2.

"You are of course free to make your own decision and we will respect that," Birch stated, with a would-be emollient smile, although there also seemed to be the hint of a threat embroidered into his tone. MI6 could and would compel him to make the right decision. For the greater good. As a means to an end. Needs must.

Before Ambler could respond in earnest, Birch excused himself to visit the toilet. Ambler wondered whether it was a strategic move, a tactical and temporary retreat. To give their conversation a fire break. For the potential handler to allow his prospective joe the time and space to come to the right conclusion. Or perhaps Birch was merely succumbing to a call of nature.

Ambler went to top up his wine but desisted on seeing his hand shake a little. The last time his hand had similarly shook had been during a dinner with his then wife, Sara. Their last supper, before divorce papers were served and he left. Had his hand shaken in anger or anxiety back then? Was his hand shaking in anger or anxiety now?

"It is for the best," Sara had posited, in relation to ending their marriage. She had been right, again.

Sara was a Catholic too (but practising), A desperate Ambler was going to argue that divorce was tantamount to sin, the undoing of a sacrament. Divorce would also cost him the earth, or at the very least his house. Part of him also still loved his wife - just not enough for him to change. Sara could have easily mentioned that adultery was a sin as well. But that had not prevented Ambler from committing it - again and again.

The author glanced around the restaurant in the hope of forgetting about Birch's proposal. His phone also vibrated, but Ambler wasn't tempted to retrieve it. He didn't want to be a slave to the device, or anything else. Aside from perhaps drink. His relationship with alcohol was either simple or complicated, depending on how sober he was. Too much was more than enough, but not having enough was worse. He could function well without alcohol in his day. But just not as well. Or as happily. To excuse or justify his crapulent behaviour Ambler had, on more than one occasion, quoted Samuel Johnson: *"He who makes a beast of himself gets rid of the pain of being a man."*

Ambler glanced outside of the large glass windows of the fine restaurant, down at the bustling scene below. He could see, but thankfully not hear, several street performers. Another figure, or struggling actor, was wearing a sandwich board. Ambler thought how people used to advertise that the "End is nigh" on them. The chap walking along the South Bank was from a shoe store, promoting that "Crocs" were on sale. Perhaps the end was nigh. Hips and summer dresses swayed. There were too many people taking selfies, to the point where it sickened Ambler and he could no longer look outside.

Granted the toilets were some distance away from their table in the far corner of the restaurant, but Birch spent as long a time in the bathroom as an Instagram model in a nightclub fixing her make-up and teasing her hair. Eventually he returned, smoothing down his eyebrows and then flattening his tie. He smiled at his friend once more, the smile of the most upmarket car salesman one could ever encounter. But a car salesman, nevertheless. Birch was not too disconcerted by his friend's response. It was only natural for any would-be operative to play hard to get, to feel fear or leverage his position. Just as it was the brief of a would-be handler to not take no for an answer. "No" meant "maybe". It might have even worried Birch if Ambler had assented too quickly - if he wanted to play the hero too much.

"I know that you are no mercenary, Daniel, but the River House has it in its gift to remunerate you for your time and trouble. You can even think of the task as a glorified author appearance - and be remunerated accordingly. I can also secure other forms of compensation in return for your service. Should the operation prove successful then it will reach the ears of the Foreign Secretary. He may even want to grant you a special audience - and give you a leg up to reach the first rung on the honours list,"

Birch asserted, believing that if Ambler were able to bring back genuine treasure, then they would all receive their just rewards.

"Meeting the Foreign Secretary may prove a punishment rather than reward. The operation is dangerous enough, without the risk of being bored to death on my return. No, I would be happy for the Foreign Secretary to cancel any meeting in favour of him spending more time with his latest mistress, rather than with me."

Birch compressed his lips in the faintest of faint smiles. He felt like he was involved in a fencing contest, but his opponent was comfortably parrying his lunges. Yet Birch believed that his old friend still wanted to answer the call. He just didn't know it yet.

Ambler regained his appetite, as soon as he saw the piece of steak in front of him. He breathed in the aroma, like a lover's perfume. He would be willing to swallow Birch's lines, if it meant he could stay and eat the well-seasoned and perfectly cooked slab of meat on his polished white plate. Steam purred up from a side order of garlic-infused broccoli. Chunks of sea salt on the twice cooked chips gleamed like uncut diamonds. Ambler savoured the taste of the morish meat, to the extent where he tuned out his dining companion. Food heaven. One of the only real heavens on earth. A moment of bliss. But the moment didn't last long, unfortunately. Unsurprisingly.

"...You can trust me, and you can trust us. You just need to trust yourself that you can do this too. You can appreciate how time is of the essence, though. We do not know the complete picture in relation to Vetrov's health. We cannot afford to allow this opportunity to die with the old man. You know yourself how combustible and changeable Vetrov can be."

Ambler merely nodded in reply but kept his own counsel whilst the two men descended into a period of silence, as they ate their lunch.

Birch just needed him to now nod in agreement, in relation to accepting the assignment. Had he hooked his fish? He would even be willing to foul hook him. Did he just need to reel him in?

"Would you like to see the dessert menu?" their French waitress asked. She smiled at Ambler once more, tucking a loose strand of blonde hair behind her ear.

"No. I'm not a sweet person," the novelist drily replied.

She laughed and smiled more freely. Birch resented his friend for effortlessly charming the girl. But he didn't show it. He had always envied his accomplished contemporary. For his girlfriends. For his grades. For his material success. For his fame. The seeds had been sown in college. He also resented his friend for never having the decency to envy him in return.

Birch would forgive Ambler for proving more popular with the comely waitress if he agreed to travel to Cuba. By the close of their lunch Ambler at least agreed to carefully consider his friend's proposal.

Maybe means yes.

3.

The two men shook hands on the South Bank, like old friends or new business partners, before going their separate ways. Birch said that he felt like going home, but in truth he would be returning to the office to brief his superior on how his meeting went.

Ambler bathed in the afternoon sun and sucked in the fresh air, as fresh as the air could be in London. For the first time, in five years, he craved a cigarette. People streamed around him, as if he were a large rock in a river. The Thames rhythmically slapped against the bank. Dirty white boats, filled with animated or obese tourists, cruised up and down, churning up streaks of foam in the dull green water. Ambler was tempted to have another drink, or three, in the nearest pub. But he decided to catch a cab and travel back to his flat in Kensington.

A number of messages flashed up on his phone as Ambler sat in the back of the taxi, as it crawled through the traffic. The first was from his agent, Alexander Ponsonby. The cocaine addict had done a sterling job over the past ten years of halving the revenue and influence of his father's prestigious literary agency. But *The Ponsonby Agency* still possessed enough marquee clients and literary estates to turn a notable profit and allow Alexander to keep dining at *Soho House* and travel to Tuscany in the Summer. The agent was the cousin of the Head of Penguin and attended Eton with the CEO of HarperCollins, so the deals still ticked over. Publishers can be more incestuous than the Welsh, and lazier than Scousers. Ponsonby had a weak chin, Hugh Grant floppy fringe and John Lennon glasses. Ambler found his agent more than slightly odious at the best of times. He was a letch, without being a drunken one, and an inveterate snob. "The good thing about Sainsbury's is that it keeps the poor people out of Waitrose," he repeatedly joked. Ambler duly tolerated the royalty cheques and advances that the agency sent him, however.

"Good news! We have secured the Norwegian deal for Keep Your Enemies Close."

Ambler would have immediately thanked and congratulated his agent if the author hadn't threatened to arrange the deal himself a fortnight ago. Ponsonby argued that the climate was tough in the country, and they were publishing fewer titles - but really the agent did not want to spend his time on a deal for such a paltry sum of money. Ambler said he would contact the publisher directly. The fear of having one his authors realise that he might not need him prompted the agent to instruct his assistant to finalise the deal.

The next message was from an editor of *The Times*, asking Ambler if he could write a piece and send it over by nine o'clock the following morning. The article would be titled, *Is Russia a Rogue State?* The editor wanted two thousand words. Ambler thought how he could have answered the question in one. *Yes.*

The literary editor of *The Tablet* emailed to ask if Ambler would be interested in reviewing a new biography of Graham Greene, called *Greene Land.* The biographer had once written a mealy-mouthed review of one of his novels. Ambler would have been willing to review *Greene Land* for free. At best he would damn the book with faint praise.

He accepted an invitation to take part in *The London History Festival*, which was conveniently being held in Kensington Central Library. The invitation had come from the festival's founder, Richard Foreman, who Ambler had drunk with on more than one occasion.

A fan had somehow got hold of his personal email address and gushed about how Ambler was his favourite author. He might have blushed at the words of praise - if he cared. The second half of the message revealed the sender's true agenda, though:

"...I would be honoured if you could read a thriller I have just completed. It's called Fire in the Whole and deals with a global conspiracy, climate change and the #MeToo movement... I have already had one beta reader call the novel "a page turner". Everyone who has read the manuscript has said that the book

should be turned into a movie too... I would be grateful if you could endorse the book and send it on to your agent and publisher. It would mean the world to me."

Ambler rolled his eyes and deleted the message.

As well as working his way through emails and replying, Ambler received a text message from his ex-wife:

"Hi, I hope you're well. I found a box of first editions of Too Soon Gone in the attic. Would you like to collect them? I will be quite busy with work this week, but I will be home tomorrow evening if convenient."

Even before the divorce Sara had been married to her work, as the deputy head of a Catholic school, Ambler considered. He had envied Sara for her faith, during their marriage, and for how happy she was in her job. Her vocation. Calling. Towards the end of their marriage Ambler would complain about how unhappy he was becoming in relation to his work:

"It's churnalism. I feel like I'm re-writing the same book each time. I'm boring myself. I'm just surprised that I'm not boring the readers."

"You should write the book on Turgenev that you always promised yourself you would," Sara replied, having patiently listened to his complaints before.

"I would not get paid as much, and it probably wouldn't sell," Ambler argued, peevishly. He also knew that the non-fiction project would involve more research and work than a spy novel.

Sara merely responded with a raised eyebrow. To others Ambler could appear as inscrutable as a sphinx, whilst to his wife he was as transparent as glass. Sara knew him too well, which was why she decided to leave him.

Ambler replied that he would pop around to the house after four o'clock the following afternoon. He fancied that he had kept his word and been far more reliable as a divorcee than he ever had been as a husband.

He yawned, again. Even breathing sometimes felt exhausting. The traffic became a blur. His eyelids felt like lead, thankfully. And thankfully he could only see darkness, rather than images of

Viktor Rybin. Ambler drifted off to sleep for a moment. But only for a moment, unfortunately. His phone vibrated and pinged once more, waking him up. No rest for the wicked. It was a message from Veronica. He had cancelled their date, having explained that he needed to attend an important lunch at the *Skylon* restaurant.

"I think my husband has found out about us. I'm worried. We shouldn't see each other for a while. Xxx."

Ambler had met the statuesque brunette in a bar in Notting Hill. She was attending a hen party. Ambler had already downed a few but was yet to quite drown out his melancholy. The conversation - and booze - flowed. He liked her figure, dress and personality - in that order. She laughed at his jokes (those which she understood). The former hairdresser was half-Irish and half-Spanish. She had been born in Wolverhampton but had thankfully lost her accent.

"I don't want to be on my own tonight," Veronica said, whispering in his ear and brushing half her body up against him, as Ambler sat on the barstool. He breathed in her perfume, which he may have liked even more than her personality.

"We're sharing a drink they call loneliness, but it's better than drinking alone," Ambler replied, although Veronica failed to note the Billy Joel reference. He subsequently found out that she liked a lady called Beyonce and a young chap named Ed Sheeran.

They went back to Ambler's flat, which was a short cab journey away. The sex was good, fuelled rather than dampened by the alcohol they consumed.

"I'm married," she confessed in the morning, though Ambler had observed the wedding ring before buying the first drinks.

He was not averse to affairs with married women. They had less time to bother him - and it was less likely that they would ever think about marrying him.

"Married is what you are, Veronica, not who you are," Ambler replied. The novelist thought it a trite line, but she seemed to like it.

They saw each other again, a week later.

"You're famous!" she almost squealed, over the dinner table. "I purchased a couple of your books. Will I get to know the real you from your novels?"

Ambler just about succeeded in suppressing his laughter.

"You may get to know part of me. Whether it's the better or worst part of me, I'll let you decide."

"I also read some articles about you. Are you a spy?" she leaned in and whispered, her eyes glinting with curiosity and desire.

"If I told you I would have to kill you, but I'd much rather kiss you, Veronica," Ambler said, before stopping her mouth with a kiss to prevent the woman from prattling on anymore.

They met for a third date. Ambler was keen to try out a new tapas restaurant in the area.

"Would you ever base a character in one of your novels on me?" Veronica asked, brushing her foot along his calf beneath the table.

"Of course," Ambler charmingly answered, seemingly enamoured - lying as much to her as he had to other women who had posed the same question over the years.

Veronica confessed how unhappy she was, being married to "Connor". He owned a few bars - and possessed more than one girlfriend. He even had a child with one of his "bits on the side".

They spent the night together. But the third time was not a charm. Veronica had initially been a cure for boredom - but now she was a cause of the disease, he fancied.

Ambler rolled his eyes and responded with another trite phrase, conveying it was for the best to end things, before deleting the message.

The black cab reached Kensington High St. He would soon be home. The afternoon remained sunnier than his mood. Ambler had welcomed the distraction of his messages, but the issue of Birch's proposal still loomed like a storm cloud on the horizon. He shifted uncomfortably in his seat - but not because of any regret or awkwardness he felt in relation to the message from Veronica. Rather he was afflicted with stiffness in his lower back again. The lack of suspension in the taxi had only aggravated things. His coccyx had fractured slightly - and the muscles had spasmed around his lower spine - as a result of being rear-ended by a classic Ferrari in Earl's Court one evening, some months ago. The young driver of the speeding vehicle suffered a cut forehead, due to a lack of airbags. They were both taken to hospital in ambulances. Ambler found out a week later that the car was not registered to the driver - and that the young boy-racer had left the country. Whether due to being intoxicated or concussed, he slurred his words when he was put into the ambulance. The insurance company was still investigating and chasing payment. Ambler's car was a write-off and he had yet to buy another. He was left with a legacy of back pain. He visited a specialist. Bought an array of overpriced orthopaedic cushions. Attended physiotherapy. He even paid for a couple of sessions with an acupuncturist, such was his desperation at one point. But still he couldn't completely shake the nagging pain, which now seemed as much a part of him as Catholic guilt. The chiropractor advised his patient that time would heal the injury. Ambler was sceptical, and not just because time hadn't cured him of his Catholic guilt over the years (Ambler couldn't forgive himself for some of his sins, so why should God?). In the same way that he drank to help wash away the guilt, Ambler regularly took painkillers to mollify his backache.

The taxi pulled up outside the *Elephant and Castle* pub on Holland Street. Ambler lived in a flat just around the corner. A barmaid waved through the window, encouraging the regular to come in. Even more than a drink now, though, Ambler wanted to take a couple of prescription painkillers. They would knock him out, but there were worse fates than oblivion.

Ambler noticed a black Range Rover, with tinted windows, slowly drive by. Its number plate started DTA - his initials. What he hadn't observed was that the vehicle had been following him since he left the restaurant.

4.

Ambler's flat may have been located in a sought-after neighbourhood in London, but few would have envied how it looked inside. Whether or not the author needed to de-clutter his life, he certainly needed to de-clutter his home. Books - new hardbacks, dog-eared paperbacks - were littered throughout every room. Stuffed vertically and horizontally into shelves. Piled precariously, Piza-like, on the floor. Ambler would claim to know where every title was, even the ones concealed beneath pieces of dirty clothing draped over them. The one- bedroom flat, which also contained a small study, came fully furnished. But Ambler had moved lots of his possessions in too, which he could not bring himself to throw away (or arrange to put into storage). Original works of art and replica prints of the likes of Vermeer, Turner and Hogarth hung on the walls, as well as lay on the floor, waiting to be put up. Coffee-stained mugs, whisky tumblers, empty wine bottles, old editions of *The Spectator* and *Literary Review* could be found in almost every room. An *Amazon Alexa* speaker rested on a dusty mahogany box, containing a pair of antique duelling pistols. Motes of dust proliferated the musty air, illuminated by the afternoon sun pouring through the windows.

Ambler made straight for the bathroom, where he swallowed a couple of painkillers. The bathroom cabinet was fuller than the fridge in the kitchen.

Every month he promised himself that he would arrange to move into a house, rather than a flat. He wanted more space, a piano, a garden. When Ambler had initially moved in, over a couple of years ago, he thought it would be temporary - partly because he believed that his wife would give him a second chance. Although, in truth, it would have been his fourth or fifth chance.

He pulled the curtains. Ambler lay on his bed, in the recovery position, to lessen the discomfort in his back. He felt like his lower spine was packed with shards of glass. It was best just to stay still and resign oneself to any pain. Thankfully, the pills were kicking in. Ambler closed his bruise-coloured eyelids. Dylan played in the background:

"I'm just going down the road, feeling bad,
Tryin' to get to heaven before they close the door."

He remained undecided about Birch's proposal. A spy novelist was as close to being a spy as Ambler ever wanted to get. "I'm a physical and moral coward," Ambler had half-joked on more than one occasion. He cursed Birch and Vetrov for involving him. *With friends like these, who needs enemies?* He couldn't unhear what was said, however. Could he really help bring down someone like Viktor Rybin? Maybe it was the pills, or the dregs of the wine in his system, but he drowsily fancied that if he could do something truly good and meaningful in the world then, perhaps, Ambler could forgive some of his sins, or at least pay a penance for them. Sleep came upon him before any decision, though.

"And all the while he was alone
The past was close behind.
He had a one too many lovers and
None of them were too refined.
All except for you.
But you were tangled up in blue."

Ambler woke in the early evening and came to a decision. He would hire a driver for the next few days. He had a number of meetings he needed to attend in London and had no wish to suffer anymore bone-shaking cab journeys. Ambler had a shortlist of one for the job: James Marshal. Ambler had been introduced to Marshal through Oliver Porter, a fellow member of his club. Oliver Porter was always impeccably well-mannered and well-dressed. Ambler thought him akin to the archetypal Englishman - and yet he was also like no one he had ever met. Porter knew plenty of higher-ups in both MI5 and MI6 - and could have well been a spy himself at some point. He was capable of both engendering trust and deceiving souls. Ambler once sat next to the convivial Porter at a club dinner and asked him what he did for a living. He replied, smiling as if enjoying a private joke, with a statement which could have concealed a multitude of sins:

"I fix things. Create solutions. Or sometimes I am paid to create problems for people."

He was still none the wiser about any details concerning Porter's chosen profession, but he was wise enough to be content not to know. Porter duly fixed the problem of arranging a driver for his fellow club member, at the time when the story of him being an alleged spy broke. Marshal proved to be a port in the storm. The former paratrooper was personable and professional. The two men shared a dry sense of humour and a love of country music. Marshal had playlists for Hank Williams, Glen Campbell and Alan Jackson. They both liked the song "Garden Party" by Ricky Nelson. Marshal seldom used ten words when one word would do, which was in stark contrast to the likes of Ambler's garrulous agent. To ward off most journalists and photographers the ex-soldier needed only to unsheathe a flinty glare. He would then sometimes turn to Ambler and offer up a roguish grin or wink. The author once inserted into a novel that a character was "like a well-read Jason Statham (which is not to say that Jason Statham might not be well read)". When he did so, he thought of Marshal. The paratrooper had served in Helmand. He had also worked as a PMC, before taking on jobs as a driver and close protection officer. Ambler never asked the driver if he had ever killed a man, partly because he was already sure of the answer.

Thankfully, Marshal never had cause to utilise his full skill set on Ambler's behalf during his different periods of employment. But Ambler often recalled witnessing the soldier in action one evening. Marshal had pulled up outside of a restaurant, to take the author home after a trade dinner. The restaurant was next to a nightclub. As Ambler got into the car, however, Marshal stepped out of it - observing how a couple of bouncers were beating up on a waif-like youth. The teenager was curled up in a ball on the ground, whilst the bouncers kicked and laughed at the poor soul. The two bouncers, one black, one white, both had broken-noses, cauliflower ears and wore long, black overcoats. Burly. Jowly.

Sniffing. Coked-up. There were a few revellers outside the club, but they pretended not to notice, for fear of not being allowed in the venue themselves. They just wanted to have a good time and avoid any unpleasantness. The soldier had a different agenda, though.

"Enough is enough," Marshal calmly and audibly remarked.

"Do yourself a favour and piss-off," one of the bouncers spat back, spittle peppering the night air.

The adolescent groaned on the floor.

Ambler's window was open. His hand was on the door handle. He was tempted to get out of the car in some show of support for Marshal or the victim - but didn't. The author wasn't wholly joking when he called himself a physical and moral coward. He hoped the situation might resolve itself on its own.

The bouncers expected the Good Samaritan to back away. But when Marshal stood his ground - and even dared to take a step forward - the larger of the two security personnel squared up to the uninvited guest.

"You want to be the next one on the ground there?" the bouncer said - or growled.

Ambler couldn't quite tell for certain, but he thought he saw Marshal break into a grin at this moment.

The bouncer followed-up his words by shoving the man he wanted to intimidate in the shoulder. Before he could draw his hand back, however, Marshal grabbed it - striking faster than a mongoose. A sickening crack of bone was quickly succeeded by a guttural howl of pain. After breaking the bouncer's hand, or arm, Marshal whipped his elbow around and connected with his opponent's face - breaking his already crooked nose. The security guard fell to the ground, groaning more than the youth.

His colleague's eyes first widened in shock and then narrowed in fury. He snorted and advanced towards the stranger, balling his two large hands into two large fists. The former boxer raised his hands and eyeballed his opponent, but as he did so Marshal raised his foot and buried it into the bouncer's groin. Whilst his victim was winded and doubled over in agony, Marshal proceeded to grab the security guard by his hair and bring his knee up into his face, rendering him unconscious. The entire encounter barely lasted a couple of minutes. Marshal's actions were deliberate and brutal. Ambler thought how the soldier had a switch, which he could turn on and off at will. God help the world if Marshal could not control the switch, he further fancied.

"I'm not sure whether trouble sometimes finds me, or I find trouble," Marshal explained, as he got back in the car. Remarkably calm, after the bloody altercation. "I just don't like bullies."

Whether it was from doing good, or enjoying the bout of violence, Ambler remembered how buoyant Marshal seemed.

Money - and the love of a good woman - saved the paratrooper. Marshal inherited a significant sum of money. He also met Grace, a former fashion model who owned a bookshop in Chiswick. Despite his comfortable and contented life, Marshal still thankfully knew how to be miserable and misanthropic every now and then, Ambler thought.

Although Marshal had officially retired, from working as a driver and close protection officer, he occasionally took the call from a few favourite clients. Ambler was, fortunately, one of them.

"Evening. Is this a good time?"

"As good a time as any. Is everything alright?" Marshal asked in a slight London accent.

"Yes. I was wondering if you could do me a favour and come out of retirement again? I could use a driver for a few days."

A slight pause.

"Can do. Grace is away, visiting friends. I could use a distraction and it'll be nice to catch-up. I can be available until this time next week."

"Great, thanks."

"You can do me a favour in return and host your next book launch at Grace's shop."

"That'll be fine. But I thought you hated the publishing tribe."

"I do. I'm only human. But Grace could use the sales and publicity for the shop. I may have to work as your driver on that night too and be made to sit in the car, so as to avoid the party."

"I'll probably have to come out and join you at some point, to avoid the throng as well. The last thing I want to hear is people telling me how talented I am. I'll message you with some details about the next few days. Thanks again, James."

"No problem. Have a nice night."

Ambler pictured his friend hanging up and reaching for a nearby whisky tumbler. With Grace away he was doubtless at home with a good book - with his dog, Violet (an adorable black and white mongrel), at his feet. Listening to country music.

The night was balmy. The curtain infrequently billowed out with a half-hearted breeze. Ambler made himself some black coffee, and swallowed a couple of muscle relaxants, as well painkillers. After messaging Marshal with his schedule, he retreated into his study to work on the article for *The Times*.

"...*The Russian Bear does not change its spots. I must admit that I too was infected with that most calamitous of diseases, hope, after the wall came down. It was the right thing to do, to extend an invitation to Russia to trade and become one happy family. But, although courted by governments and corporations alike, Russia never really joined the new world order. Moscow rules still eclipsed the rule of law. A kleptocracy was a far more profitable form of government than democracy. The KGB became the FSB - but it was still the same old Cheka. The new boyars - of the likes of Roman Abramovich and Alisher Usmanov - just served a new tzar. Putin. Allegedly... Bill Clinton and Tony Blair believed that they were powerful and charming enough to bring Putin into line. They thought that he was a man they could do business with, as Thatcher had done with Gorbachev. Surely Putin would see the light, it was just a matter of time. They were even gracious enough to turn a blind eye to certain misdemeanours, such as war crimes in Chechnya, because they judged that Russia could put away its ricin-tipped umbrellas for good. They believed that Russia would assist in combating*

DUTY CALLS

Islamic terrorism, the threat of an emboldened Tehran, the instability in Syria. "Putin has enormous potential," Bill Clinton once remarked. Adding, "I think he's very smart and thoughtful. I think we can do a lot of good with him." Tony Blair was similarly taken in by Putin. Or surely the former Prime Minister wasn't lying to us when he pronounced that, "Vladimir Putin is a leader who's ready to embrace a new relationship with the European Union and the United States." And let us not forget George W. Bush's endorsement: "President Putin's leadership offers hope to Russia and the whole world." But Russia remained part of the problem that the west grappled with, not its solution. International law is a punchline to Russia. As much as the west - and certain western leaders - should feel ashamed and appalled for past errors in judgement, we should duly spend more time looking to the future and the conflicts to come... Russia, or perhaps more so Putin, still pines for a Soviet Union. The rogue state will have few qualms about becoming a rogue empire."

The dead of night. The breeze was blessingly cooler. Ambler rubbed his tired eyes, thinking how if only one of his film-optioned novels could go to first day's filming, when he would finally get paid proper money, then he could give up such hack work for a year. He was weary of newspaper editors asking him to comment on a world that he scarce cared about. If he chased his agent or the film company, they would just reply that the project was "in development". Ambler half-jokingly thought to himself how his whole life was "in development" - and that ultimately nothing would come of it.

His back started to ache again, and Ambler craved sleep even more than sex.

Morning. Ambler experienced all of a moment's respite, after he woke, before he was mired in the thought of Birch's proposal once more. He felt like there was a paving slab, or two, weighing on his chest. He was not sure if even whisky could burn away the acrid taste in his mouth. Today was the day to decide. The clock was ticking. But it had always been ticking. It was now significantly louder. Ambler had no qualms about letting his old friend down. He just didn't want to let himself down. Although he could, of course, live with that too.

He checked his phone. A message from his editor at *The Times* thanked him for the piece and said he would be in touch about a follow-up article. In the past Ambler would have felt flattered and engaged. But he was anything but. The habit of a freelancer is to always say "yes". He just wasn't sure anymore if it was a good or bad habit.

Ambler more than half-smiled when he saw a message from Samantha Stiles appear on the screen.

"Hi, I will be flying into London tomorrow for a few days. Are you free to meet? I can be free for dinner or the theatre. You can have me for dessert, or an encore, too. X."

Images of Viktor Rybin were replaced by the American journalist. Her gym-toned figure. Long, glossy blonde hair. Wide, whitened smile. Expensive cocktail dresses and equally expensive heels and lingerie sets. Samantha was manna from heaven. The New Yorker came to London every few months. They would go out for dinner or see a play - and then spend the night with one another in her hotel suite. It was always an enjoyable evening. The financial journalist, who had worked for *Goldman Sachs* and *Bloomberg*, considered herself an alpha-female. A self-titled "Mistress of the Universe". She was originally from California, but intelligent. In some ways Samantha treated Ambler like he was a mere plaything, a distraction. Sometimes he minded, but most of the time he didn't. She seldom bored him, aside from when she quoted Ayn Rand or name-dropped celebrities, but that was probably because they spent so little time together. A friend of Ambler's once met Samantha in the foyer of a *The Old Vic*, just before a production of *A Streetcar Named Desire*. His mouth was agape, his eyes bulging like a cartoon character. He called her "perfect - a ten", whilst all but salivating. Ambler nodded in agreement, uncomfortably proud. But she still wasn't Sara, he lamented.

Ambler was tempted to reply that he was available. Would it be the worst crime in the world to lock himself away in a hotel room with the voracious woman and forget about Viktor Rybin and Yevgeny Vetrov? But something prevented him from committing to the tryst.

"I'll let you know as soon as I can. Sorry, I may have something on."

He regretted having accepted the lunch invitation with Birch. But MI6 were not accustomed to taking no for an answer.

They will probably use a stick, if the carrot doesn't work.

5.

It was another fine day, although Ambler felt that the sun wasn't particularly shining in his heart.

The two men had not seen one another for over a year, but neither was prone to sentiment. They merely offered each other a brief nod and half-smile as an initial greeting. Although Marshal had only been asked to act as a driver, the ex-soldier's eyes still flitted about, searching for possible threats. "Habit makes more converts than reason," Tom Paine, ironically perhaps, once wrote. The former paratrooper may have lost his soldierly gait, but he hadn't entirely lost his soldierly build. Ambler couldn't quite decide if Marshal should be described as an immovable object or an unstoppable force. He could be quick to smile and laugh, when drinking or in the right company, but he still possessed an infantryman's thousand-yard stare and sentry-like demeanour on occasion. Marshal wore jeans, a navy suit jacket, an ironed light-blue shirt and polished shoes (with rubber rather than leather souls, so he never lost his footing).

Ambler noticed the headline in a folded over newspaper in the front seat, which Marshal had been reading: *Russia's New World Order*! Part of him wanted to read the corresponding piece, but most of him didn't. Although it was still morning, Ambler already felt exhausted. Weathered.

The car was a Jaguar. Marshal had cleaned the interior that morning, albeit a faint smell of dog still lingered in the air, from when he and Grace took their dog Violet to the park.

"So, what have you been up to?" Ambler asked, wondering if his friend was now engaged - or had decided on a new career.

"Nothing much," Marshal replied, with an unassuming shrug and habitual poker-face. Although it would have been of interest to the thriller writer, Marshal had no intention of recounting his run-ins with the Albanian mafia and a former IRA terrorist during the past year or two. Oliver Porter had helped the soldier fix the problems. Suffice to say they were now dead issues. "And is there anything new in your life?"

Ambler thought about broaching the subject of Birch's proposal. Unburdening himself. Perhaps confiding in Marshal had been part of the reason why he had hired him. He was a penitent in need of a priest.

"No. There's nothing new under the sun."

They set off. Ambler asked if Marshal could put on the air conditioning. He didn't mind letting the air in through the open window, but he could do without the iniquitous sounds. Most people would have enjoyed living in Kensington. But Ambler found the opulence somewhat vulgar and garish. He preferred his old house in Greenwich, close to the river.

As well as the air conditioning, the driver also switched on some music:

"...The hard roads are the ones worth choosing..."

The seats and suspension were welcome. He tapped his pockets again, to make sure the strips of painkillers were there. Muscle spasms could strike at any time, like religious despair.

A message came through on his phone, which sent a jolt through his body or being. A Russian cultural institute, based in St Petersburg, were extending an invitation for the author to give a talk on Pushkin. Ambler may not have been a spy, but he was suddenly gripped by a spy's paranoia. Did the Russians already know about Vetrov and himself? Was he being lured into a trap? Birch said that he ran a tight ship - but MI6 had a lamentable history of being a leaky ship. The ghost of Kim Philby still haunted its corridors. Ambler's pulse raced. He shifted in his seat - and it had nothing to do with back pain. For a moment or two he seemed to stop breathing. If Marshal's eyes would have been on his passenger instead of the road, he would have noticed something amiss. But as Ambler scrolled down the message he finally breathed out. He read the entire thread of the exchange and realised that he had first been in discussions with the institute a year ago. It was just a coincidence that they were finalising things now. But "a spy should never believe in coincidences," Ambler had written in one of his novels. His hand shook a little as he kindly replied that he would not be able to make the proposed date for the event - but would be in touch when his schedule was freer. It was important to be polite, even when receiving a possible death threat.

"And he just walked along, alone
With his guilt so well concealed
And muttered underneath his breath
"Nothing is revealed.""

When Ambler first released his spy novels his publishers were based in a large riverfront building on the Strand. Since the crash of 2008, however, most publishers and agents had scaled down their real estate costs. They moved away from W1 and headed further east. His publishers were now based in the perfectly fine, but less prestigious area, of Blackfriars.

"Good luck," Marshal remarked, all but winking, as he dropped his client off outside the grand-ish entrance to the building. He knew how little Ambler enjoyed attending meetings with his paymasters. The author had conveniently forgotten to tell his agent about the catch-up meeting, lest he attend and contribute pointless comments or superfluous questions to the conversation.

Ambler was greeted with number two smiles from the reception staff (their number one smiles were reserved for the fully-fledged celebrities, with more than half a million social media followers). He was given a pass and frayed lanyard. He was tempted to take the stairs as the lift was fully automated, which for some reason he didn't like. Perhaps it was due to the lack of freedom and control.

The open plan office was not entirely a hive of activity. It was a sunny day, so a good portion of staff were coincidentally choosing to work from home. Others were off sick with unpredictable and unprovable migraines - or extending their maternity leave. Ambler knew that there were a good few individuals at his publishing house who were worth their weight in gold (or at least silver). Most of the people Ambler now observed, though, were just dully staring at their computer screens, checking out their *Facebook* accounts and watching *YouTube* clips of cats. The pale-faced, earnest editorial assistant who led Ambler to the meeting room wore expensive pumps and a shapeless t-shirt emblazoned with the slogan, *"Trans Women Are Women"*. He seemed to remember that she wore a top before with *"Capitalism Kills"* on it, as she took selfies on her iPhone. *All is vanity under the sun. Now there's a message for a t-shirt*, Ambler mused. The silly girl, the daughter of the finance director at the company, had probably never heard of Viktor Rybin (and had no idea of Putin's crimes), Ambler also thought.

The meeting room was glass-fronted and home to a long, ugly aluminium table. The walls were lined with bookcases. Someone had been mindful enough to place some of Ambler's titles face out. They would doubtless change them back after he left. He was offered a glass of expensive water, still or sparkling. He would have preferred a measure of cheap wine, but it had recently become a "dry building". *For shame.*

Fortunately, Ambler was quickly greeted by a familiar, welcome face. His veteran editor, Tim Powell, was considered a dinosaur in the trade - but that was why Ambler liked him. Powell had a pronounced paunch and round, amiable countenance (which was often marked with tiny specks of blood from cutting himself shaving). More than one joke had been made about Powell appearing to be pregnant (but the editor had made most of the jokes himself). He was perennially tucking in his shirt and collecting food stains on an array of similar looking ties. Powell reminded Ambler of Terry Jones from *Monty Python*. The self-deprecating editor enjoyed a drink - and politically incorrect joke. Despite being excellent at his job, publishing (like other industries in the media) was as inherently ageist as it was racist. The publishing house (which seemed to be turning more and more into a student common room) had encouraged Powell to retire on several occasions, but the "progressive" higher-ups half his age were unable to sack him due to the fact that a number of bestselling authors, including Ambler, would never sign a contract with them again if they did.

Unfortunately, they were soon joined by Tamara Fallon, the marketing director for the imprint. Tamara had thin lips and an even thinner smile. She looked like a cross between Jacinda Ahearn and Victoria Beckham, if one can imagine such a creature. Tamara prided herself in being "on trend" a lot, whatever that meant. She was often coming back from holidaying in Sorrento, Seville, or Mumbai ("You can't ever say Bombay!") with her "life partner". The places she visited tended to be "very unique" and "cosmopolitan". She had never travelled north of the Cotswolds, though. Ambler had never known Tamara not to insert into a conversation that it was all about "Human rights, not wrongs". He suspected that Powell poured whisky into his coffee to help him get through the multiple meetings she arranged with the editor, so they could be "on the same page". The marketing director needed to take the spy novelist aside a couple of months ago, to have a "delicate discussion" as she called it. Ambler had "misgendered" one of her team and caused offence.

"Pronouns are important," she told the author, placing her palm on her chest to somehow enhance the seriousness of the issue.

Not even Grace was this passive aggressive, in her prime, Ambler thought to himself, whilst enduring the lecture. He refused to apologise. The marketing director brought the "incident" up with the CEO, but was told to drop any grievance. The CEO did not want to give a bestselling author a reason to join a rival. The desire to make money still rightly trumped the desire to satisfy certain conceits in publishing. But the gap was narrowing.

The meeting commenced in earnest. Ambler was first presented with the draft of a mock-up cover for his next novel, *The Quiet Englishman*. The cover was as suitably derivative as the title, Ambler fancied. "We are happy with it. It's quite unique," Tamara asserted, with a lack of irony, tapping away on her iPad like a piano.

DUTY CALLS

Ambler tapped his foot impatiently beneath the table. He was anxious to get the meeting over and done with and have a drink. Perhaps he was frustrated with himself, that he still hadn't made a decision in relation to Birch's proposal.

"Paperback sales for *Russian Roulette* have been strong. Our research shows that you are gaining more female readers," she remarked, her voice somehow tinged with confoundment or disappointment. "You may want to consider increasing the romance levels in your next novel."

The woman couldn't put an outfit together, let alone sentence, Ambler mused. The literature graduate had once boasted that she had been able to get through her degree without having once read any Shakespeare or Chaucer. She was not going to tell him how to write.

"It could be the case that I have gained more female readers because, and not in spite of, the lack of romance in my books," Ambler argued, as passive aggressive as his ex-wife, whilst forcing a civil smile.

Tamara's features tightened and she compressed her lips. The self-titled liberal - who regularly wore different charity wristbands, branded her social media with all manner of flags and ran "diversity days" - did not like it when people disagreed with her. The meeting was almost becoming an unsafe space.

Powell wryly smiled into his coffee mug, amused by the comment.

"Now, let us come to social media," the marketeer announced, her voice becoming shriller and schoolmarmish. "I still do not believe you have embraced all relevant platforms. You really will be able to connect to a community of other readers and writers. I have even created a special list of emoticons for our authors. They are a great shorthand for telling people how you feel."

Ambler and Powell shared a look and rolled their eyes.

Tamara Fallon could read Sally Rooney, but not the room.

The author and his editor shared a bottle of Pinot Noir at *El Vino's* in Blackfriars. They had both let out a sigh of relief, or exasperation, after the meeting. Ambler joked that he might have to arrange a dentist appointment - and root canal work - to get him out of the next one.

The wine bar was turning a healthy trade. There were plenty of tables filled with overweight middle-aged men working in law, finance or insurance, buying each other lunch on expenses. They chortled and slapped tables, animated by the endless bottles of red they consumed. Ambler cast an eye over his fellow diners. He observed plenty of mid-priced suits and mid-priced (or more) shoes. They still read The Times, but online. They had paid off most of their mortgage - and they could afford to send their children to Russell Group universities. They had friends who owned holiday homes in France and Italy. They're wives were still young enough to get away with dying their hair blonde. They could afford to buy a Rolex, but only the models at the lowest price points. Many felt trapped in a job they resented, or by a wife they couldn't afford to divorce. They envied and resented anyone more successful than them, and scorned those they considered beneath them. But there were some who rightly felt self-satisfied with their lives. Within a couple of years they might feel a twinge or two of angina, if they were not already on statins. Ambler hated himself for such ungenerous thoughts towards others. A lapsed Catholic was surely not supposed to feel such acute guilt. But guilt was good. Guilt meant that he wasn't an atheist or, worse, an Anglican. Ambler was also heartened by observing lots of paperback books poking out of suit pockets. His fellow diners devoured books, as well as claret - and were all the happier and better for it. *"The proper study of mankind is books,"* Ambler thought, recalling the quote from Aldous Huxley. He also remembered how one of the greatest moments in his life came when he was sitting on a train and the passenger opposite was reading one of his novels. Such was the high that Ambler experienced, he missed his stop.

"Any thoughts as to what you would like to write about next?" Powell asked, savouring the taste of the rich Pinot Noir and popping an olive in his mouth. "There's no immediate rush, though."

Ambler paused and took a mouthful of wine too. He liked and trusted his editor. He was a friend. For a moment he appeared like he was going to say something important or meaningful. For a moment Powell thought that something was wrong. But then Ambler merely replied:

"I was flirting with the idea of setting a story in Cuba. I've not quite settled on things yet, but I may arrange a short research trip to Havana. My accountant will be able to write it off as a tax break."

"If Nixon could go to China, Daniel Ambler can go to Cuba. Where else should you go, but into the lion's den? I'd still recommend that, no matter where the setting may be, you put together another cold war thriller. Follow the sales, as well as the sun. The old enemy is the new enemy. The only way to stand up to the Russian Bear is to stand up to the Russian Bear. Your novels are able to shine a light on the darkness. Provide light and heat. Not enough people are aware of what Putin has done or is doing. It's state sponsored gangsterism," Powell argued, becoming untypically animated. "Putin and his band of menacing men have duped us. He certainly duped Tony Blair, who still has few qualms in relation to duping others. I was talking to an author the other day who said that there was already a plan in place for Russia to invade Ukraine, or rather further invade Ukraine. They will post forces on the border of the country and claim that they are merely running military exercises. The Russians will use Belarus as a proxy too. The Russian army will utilise, ironically or not, blitzkrieg tactics to reach Kiev and unseat Zelensky. Putin believes in a Russian Empire and he is hellbent on expanding its borders, back to old Soviet Union levels. He is already on record saying that he does not believe that Ukraine is a real country. He is intent on bringing Ukraine into the Russian family of nations, kicking and screaming if need be. Rumour has it that Putin is gravely ill - and wants to write himself into the history books before he dies (just as Hitler invaded Russia prematurely because he wanted to defeat his enemies before he met his demise). Usually when men try to write themselves into the history books, they do so in blood. In the same way that the German plan to invade France before the Great War was named after its author, Schlieffen, the plan to invade Ukraine is being named after its architect, one Viktor Rybin. And as this Rybin drafts his plan the west appears content to compose a suicide note, as it ignores the writing on the wall."

Ambler coughed and spluttered on hearing the Russian's name, as his wine went down the wrong hole. His face reddened, resembling the colour of the drink he spilled. Heads turned towards their table. A waitress fetched the customer a glass of water. The prospective spy reined himself in, eventually. Glibness returned. Normal service was resumed.

"I'm not sure about wanting to write myself in the history books. I'd just like the legacy of keeping most of my novels in print. Or even just half of them. If I show God that I'm not greedy He may then be more inclined to answer my prayers."

"And how's the back?" Powell said, noticing his friend sitting uncomfortably in his chair as the editor ate another olive. All but wincing a couple of times. His author appeared like a man in need of the toilet. Perhaps his coughing fit had triggered a spasm.

"It's been worse, but it's certainly been better too. It's marginally less irritating than Tamara."

"That bad then?"

"I'm still popping pills like you're popping olives into your mouth. Time heals most wounds, though, I'm hoping."

"Did they ever track down the cretin who ran into the back of you?"

"No, I don't think so. He left the country. It's all in the past now, aside from the backache. I'm tempted to have my next protagonist suffer from a spinal injury, as I've already done the research. Some good should come out of this misery," Ambler replied, half-smiling and drinking his wine as his phone vibrated in his pocket. He wondered if it was Samantha, responding to his message. He hoped it wasn't Veronica. He was content to consign that affair to the past as well.

Ambler, along with various other spy novelists, had been guilty of writing in one of his books of how a vehicle "gunned" its way through the capital. In reality, a car can only crawl through central London traffic. They were currently inching through Temple, on their way to *Waterstone's* in Leadenhall Market for a stock signing. He stared out of the window, squinting a little in the sunlight. The scene was thick with exhaust fumes, history and affluence. Amber noticed one barrister, marching purposefully or triumphantly down the street, his robes billowing in the breeze - his wig slightly, comically, askew. A paragon of self-importance and satisfaction. His skin was tanned, almost varnished. Perhaps he had just won a case. Perhaps he had just billed someone for two hours, when he had only worked for sixty-one minutes.

Ambler was only half observing the world outside, however. His thoughts turned to his "friend" Yevgeny Vetrov. Men are vain creatures. But wealthy and powerful men, at the end of their lives, can be vainer. Ambler wondered if Vetrov was requesting an audience with the author to ask him to write his biography. Vetrov had pitched the idea previously. The oligarch could tell himself that he would live on through the book, take revenge on his enemies. Attack them from the grave. People can be vindictive, as well as vain, Ambler idly mused. But should Vetrov make such a proposal, how would he respond? Every writer has their price.

"How was your meeting?" Marshal asked.

"It could have and should have been shorter... I just waited for the marketing director to say her piece, and then went for a drink with my editor to discuss things in earnest."

"You should try attending a meeting in the army with the equivalent of your marketing director. You need the patience of a saint to grin and bear being lectured to by someone who talks a lot, but has nothing to say. You are taught more about how to tweet appropriately than shoot accurately nowadays, I warrant.

But soldiers are seldom saints," the former para asserted, having never regretted either joining or leaving the regiment.

They reached Leadenhall Market in the City of London, full of men in suits and women in heels. Ambler popped into a small supermarket and purchased a couple of bottles of wine and some chocolates, to give to the bookshop. Small acts of kindness were important. Ambler hoped that they all added up, as grand gestures such as remaining faithful as a husband or travelling to Cuba to help save the world were likely to be beyond him.

Ambler never refused a stock signing request in London. He was always grateful when a bookseller or shop championed his titles. It was flattering (and should he one day receive a decent royalty rate, it might even be profitable). The author remembered his time working in a bookshop. He enjoyed meeting certain authors. They had been generous with their time and advice.

The pale, bespectacled bookseller who greeted the semi-famous author was a little nervous, but Ambler put him at ease. No doubt he had met demanding writers in the past who were delusional about their place in the world. Literary novelists. Underappreciated geniuses. Celebrities promoting ghost written novels. Ambler asked for a glass of water and said he would be fine to be left on his own. A healthy pile of books sat on a table, and he started to work his way through them.

As had happened in the past, the author was approached by more than once curious customer. Some purchased a book for themselves - or bought a signed and dedicated copy as a gift for a family member or friend. Ambler told himself to grin and bear it as he was asked various, ubiquitous questions:

"Have you ever thought about turning one of your books into a film?... How long does it take you to write a novel?... Have you ever read any John le Carré?"

After he finished signing the stock, Ambler had a brief browse around the shop and made a few purchases. He picked up a copy of *Checkmate in Berlin*, by Giles Milton, for Marshal and bought a newly published biography of Ada Lovelace for his ex-wife. Ambler also purchased a copy of *Red Heat: Conspiracy, Murder and the Cold War in the Caribbean* by Alex von Tunzelmann for himself, just in case he needed something to read on a long flight to Cuba.

Marshal was parked outside.

"Where to now?" he asked.

"Home. Greenwich," Ambler replied, without thinking. The slightly amused or confused expression on the soldier's face prompted Ambler to explain his answer. "Sorry, I need to visit Sara and collect some books."

The divorcee rolled his eyes and made a face, but in truth he was looking forward to seeing his ex-wife.

6.

Greenwich. Home. Or what had been his home. Or what would never be his home again - although the writer sometimes created scenarios which climaxed in a reconciliation. A happy ending.

Ambler had originally bought the house, which was more of a cottage, to be away from the chattering classes. The literary scene. He purchased the property because Sara liked it, because it was old, because it possessed a fireplace and garden. Because it was close to the river. Ambler would often sit on a bench on the bank of the Thames and enjoy the silence and stillness of the river, reading Chekhov or plotting a novel.

The ivy still climbed up the old brickwork, like capillaries spreading throughout the body. The rose bushes were well-kept and in bloom. *No rose without a thorn but many a thorn without a rose,* Ambler thought, recalling the quote by Schopenhauer. He could still smell the thyme in the herb garden. Rumour had it that Ford Maddox Ford had rented the cottage one summer and invited Joseph Conrad to stay. But Ambler knew better than to believe too much in mere rumour. The property was intended to be a family home. Sara suffered a miscarriage, a year after they moved in. Something inside of Ambler broke and never healed properly. He hated God or the world for being cruel. The author, prone to self-absorption, sometimes imagined that he would be as bad a father as he was a husband, though.

"Are you sure that you don't want to come in? Sara would doubtless like to see you again," Ambler said, turning back towards his driver, after swallowing the mint he'd sucked on to disguise any trace of wine on his breath.

"I'll say hello later, when I pick you up. Just message me when you're ready. I need to call Grace and check in with the dog sitter, over a pint in the pub we just went by. A man's work is never done."

Ambler instinctively reached for the key in his pocket but then checked himself. It wasn't his place anymore, quite literally, to invite himself in. Curtains twitched in the windows of the houses flanking his. He had got on well with his former neighbours and been a popular regular in the local pub. He had made a home for himself in the neighbourhood. But, quite rightly, people had sided with Sara during the divorce. He was a "philanderer". He did not own the energy to be a "narcissist", but that did not or would not stop critics from calling him one.

Sara opened the door. Smiling warmly. Genuinely. She was still admirably and annoyingly beautiful. Julie Christie in the late seventies/early nineteen eighties. He breathed in her perfume. On more than one occasion Ambler had bought the same scent as a gift for girlfriends. She was dressed casually in a polka dot blouse and a white, linen A-line skirt. Perhaps she wore it because she knew that Ambler preferred it when she wore pencil skirts, which clung to her enviable figure. His ex-wife could look attractive in almost anything, maybe even crocs. She looked good for forty. Too good. Life begins at forty, some say. Sara's life may have begun after divorcing Ambler. The gimlet-eyed author immediately noticed that her skin was glowing more than normal. Tanned. Had she recently been on holiday? Who with? She had mentioned a couple of months ago in passing, innocently or otherwise, that she was seeing someone. Had they gone away together? Ambler wanted his ex-wife to be happy, but not in love. Not too happy.

"Come in."

She said, I'll give you shelter from the storm, Ambler thought, quoting Dylan. There were times when he had played *Blood on the Tracks* on a loop, during and after the divorce.

"Thanks."

The writer's eyes moved around the house, noting any new changes, as Ambler followed Sara through the hallway and into the kitchen. Slowly but surely *their* home was becoming *her* home. He passed the doorway to her study (which had once been his study). The room now looked significantly airier and tidier. There was a new Persian rug on the floor. A new antique brass lamp. Had she and her "someone" been antiquing together, as they had once done when first married? Ambler also noticed how a print of a Caspar David Friedrich painting had been moved from their (or her) bedroom to downstairs. She used to keep a wedding photo by her bedside table. Was it still there? He was tempted to use the upstairs bathroom at some point, sneak into her room and check.

The kitchen was the same but different. There hadn't been any major work since the divorce, but the space was cleaner and roomier. There were no coffee rings on the oak dining table, no overflowing ashtrays, no empty wine glasses, no half-read newspapers splayed about the place.

"Would you like something to drink? A coffee, wine or beer?" she said, tucking a lock of blonde hair behind her ear. One of the prettiest sights in the world, for Ambler. She smiled again too. Her full, wide mouth could smile in a loving, amused, wry or mischievous fashion.

"A beer would be great, thanks. I've hired Marshal again to drive me around for a few days."

"And how is James? It would have been fine to invite him in," Sara replied, whilst retrieving a bottle of beer and frosted glass from the fridge. Did she know that Ambler would choose a beer? She knew him well. Too well.

"He may pop in when he collects me. He said that he wants to catch-up with Grace, over the phone," Ambler remarked, before gulping down half the bottle of beer, which he had poured into his glass.

"I'm glad he's still with her. She's good for him. Are they engaged yet?"

Ambler recalled how plenty of friends had mentioned how Sara was good for him when they first started seeing one another. There had been plenty of other people who doubtless advised her that she was better off without him when they separated.

"There's a part of Marshal which would rather sign-up to the army again than sign a marriage register, but you never know."

"And how's your day been?"

"I had a meeting at the publishers. The good news is that I caught up with Tim. The bad news is that I had to attend a meeting with a marketing director, who was able to inspire a heady mixture of tedium and irritation in her audience. Thankfully, I could barely hear what she was saying over the sound of her virtue signalling. Tim told me that she is petrified that news may come out that, two years ago, she hired a black cleaner - and she will be judged a modern-day slaver. She also fired the cleaner, after accusing her of stealing. Fortunately, my sales are as strong as my dislike of her," Ambler said, drily or drolly.

Sara tilted her head back and laughed freely. Teeth gleaming. Her fingertips stroked her neck as she did so. Ambler had once been the one to caress her throat in such a way. Her nails were manicured, polished and tipped. Her laugh was one of the most attractive sounds in the world, for Ambler. His foot started to tap beneath the table once more. Was it from frustrated desire? Or was the anxiety of getting back to Birch with his decision still lurking in the back of his mind, edging forward with all the subtlety of a creeping barrage during the Great War?

"I know the type, unfortunately. The teaching profession has been infected with over-earnestness far more than publishing. The Roundheads outnumber the Cavaliers. We had a new, zealous teacher just the other day bring up how "white" and "elitist" Shakespeare and Jane Austen were. She proposed that we should remove them from the syllabus to make us more "relevant". The lunatics are taking over the asylum. Perhaps there is no other sound to be heard nowadays in the teaching profession but virtue signalling," Sara remarked, her smooth brow creased in disgruntlement.

Ambler seldom saw Sara angry, or even disgruntled (aside from when she found out about his affair, or rather affairs). As much as Ambler had been a cause of unhappiness in the past, he did not like to see his ex-wife unhappy now.

"I'm not sure that I have the time, moral authority or energy to virtue signal," Ambler commented, with a befuddled expression. He was pleased to see the tension in her face dissipate, as she gently smiled. Sara also noticed his beer running low and wordlessly, kindly fetched him another from the fridge.

"How's your back by the way?"

"Better, thank you. I'm even more ill-suited to carry the weight of the world on my shoulders, though."

After the accident Sara had offered to take time off work to look after Ambler for a few days. He was tempted to take her up on the offer. But pills, rather than love or affection, are the best medicine. She did generously buy him a new, expensive chair for his study which alleviated his discomfort. She still cared about him. But care wasn't love. Or sex. But it was more than he deserved. She was still too good for him.

"Well, if you need help carrying the weight of your books, let me know. I've left them in a box in the hallway. I found myself reading the novel again the other day. I also found myself crying again. It really is a beautiful book," Sara remarked, honestly. "You will also be proud of me, in that I quoted Pushkin the other day. "Receive with indifference both flattery and slander, and do not argue with a fool." It's increasingly difficult not to find oneself arguing with a fool of late, however. More so in the staffroom than in any class with children."

God, she was beautiful, wise and witty, Ambler thought to himself. And he had hurt her - and damned himself by ruining their marriage. He wanted to tell her how proud of her he was, for so many other reasons. For improving the education of countless children over the years. For keeping her faith. For leaving him. He would have liked to apologise to her for making her cry, for reasons unrelated to his novel.

Ambler stared at her for a moment. Like he used to. Enamoured. Grateful. Dumbstruck. Sara's phone rang. Ambler jolted a little, as if suddenly being woken up. She checked the caller ID and answered. After listening to what the person at the other end of the line said, for about a minute, Sara remarked to Ambler,

"Sorry, duty calls. It's a colleague. One of the school governors is pushing to expel a student. He's a good boy, though. Everyone deserves a second chance. I'll take the call in another room. I shouldn't be too long."

Duty calls.

Birch had said the phrase in earnest, but it came across as a joke. Sara had used it as a throwaway term, but her words somehow lodged themselves in the remnants of his conscience. He recalled a speech that Sara once gave at a prize giving event at her school:

"...Duty and honour are not just words. They are part of the vocabulary of the soul. Should you pile such words up - and the deeds which they inspire - they may one day reach heaven..."

At the time, Ambler fancied that the speech was somewhat trite and conceited. He still did. But...

A couple of sparrows darted through the air, out in the garden, and landed on the birdfeeder hanging from a small cherry tree. The lawn was as manicured as her nails.

His phone vibrated in his pocket, with a message. Ambler took another swig of beer. It may have been Birch, chivvying him up for an answer. Or it may have been Samantha, with a far more attractive proposal. It would likely be neither. An anti-climax. Life was like that. He decided to refrain from checking the phone for now. He wanted to remain frozen in time, with a cold drink.

He could hear Sara in the other room, although he could not quite work out what she was actually saying. *Sara.* Perhaps if he completed his mission, or even just if he failed to complete it, he would finally be good enough for her. Worthy. Even if it was just for one day. Even if he could never tell her what he had done. His heart pounded, as if it were a prisoner hitting iron bars, trying to get out. Ambler breathed a little quicker. He even, for a moment, had problems swallowing - until he gulped down some more beer. He was frightened, because he had made his decision. Birch would be happy, albeit that was one of the last reasons why he would message to accept his offer. Ambler wondered when he had last made such a leap of faith. Had it been after graduating, when he turned down a job in the City to work as a bookseller and write his first biography? Unlike many of his peers, Ambler came from a modest background. He was the son of a postman, who had earned scholarships and bursaries, whilst working part-time to support himself. Success was far from assured.

Sara returned, to observe her ex-husband staring intently out of the window, picking at the label of his sweating bottle of beer. She knew him well enough, or too well, to realise that Ambler was pre-occupied. He looked like he had just received the news that a friend had died.

"Is something wrong?"

"No, surprisingly," Ambler replied, with a wan or wistful smile, before retrieving his phone.

The message was from Marshal.

"Ready when you are."

Ambler was ready. Just about.

7.

"Where to now?" Marshal said, after saying goodbye to Sara. He had always liked Ambler's former wife. Not many people were an alloy of elegance and fun. He could appreciate why his friend had cause to kick himself for losing her. It was unlikely he would find someone else like Sara.

"I think I deserve a drink or three. How about we head back to Kensington? I'll shout you a pint in the *Elephant & Castle*."

Ambler could still feel the sensation on his cheek from where Sara lightly kissed him. He messaged Birch. In order to initiate his potential joe into a cloak and dagger world, the handler had instructed the spy novelist to deploy a code phrase to signify his assenting to the operation.

"I can make dinner next month."

Within the time that Ambler puffed out his cheeks, sighed and checked to reply to any urgent emails, Birch replied:

"Excellent. Good man. I'll be in touch."

Ambler couldn't remember the last time that someone had deemed him a "good man". It would have meant more if it had come from anyone but Simon Birch, he fancied.

The pub was authentic enough, for Kensington. Kensington was still London, one could argue. Although one could argue that London was no longer London, for better or worse. Marshal craved more than one drink too - and Ambler offered the driver his sofa for the night. The soldier accepted. He had slept in more uncomfortable places, including behind a rock in Helmand with the Taliban not a hundred yards away, keen on killing him.

The two men entered the dimly lit establishment. The décor was nothing to write about. Staff and patrons alike gave a nod and half-smile to the regular. The barmaid, Kitty, offered up a smile to the ruggedly handsome stranger he was with as well.

Marshal scanned the scene. There was a couple in the corner, in gym clothes, as attractive and vacuous as social media

51

influencers. They tapped away on their phones, rather than spoke to each other. One of them rubbed their hands with Purell, checked their reflection in the mirror and squealed with delight on receiving a message - and that was just the man. A tweed-suited old gent, smelling of lavender and stout, sat on a barstool and read a well-thumbed copy of *Flashman and the Great Game*. One can find a better class of sot in Kensington. A quartet of clean-shaven hedge fund managers, in crisply ironed sky-blue shirts and mustard corduroy trousers, occupied another corner. Over the course of the evening, they would talk about property prices, ski resorts, bonuses, golf and how the local library was attracting "undesirable looking people". The more they drank the duller they became.

Ambler paid for a couple of beers, which would have been half the price in the area where Marshal still owned a flat. The Elephant & Castle.

They found as quiet an alcove as possible and sat down. The cool lager ran down his parched throat. It would have been worth the cost, at twice the price. Ambler still didn't quite know if alcohol fuelled the flames, like pouring petrol on a fire, of his world-weariness or if it dampened them. He was still willing to carry out the ongoing experiment.

"Sara looked well. She enjoyed her holiday, it seems," Marshal remarked.

So she had been on holiday. Ambler was tempted to ask if Marshal knew whether she went away with anyone. But it was important to convey to the world, and himself, that it was over. Sara didn't matter to him. She was part of his past. Marshal and Sara had caught-up with one another whilst Ambler went upstairs to use the toilet. He also snuck into her bedroom to see whether their wedding photo still took pride of place. It did. He still wasn't completely just a part of her past.

"Yes. The honeymoon of divorce never ends."

"Do you ever think that you will marry again?"

"Never say never. The only absolute is that there are no absolutes. But there may be a greater chance of you going back to

Afghanistan. My accountant would advise me against remarrying too, for fear of divorcing again. I wouldn't wish to put you off, though. Have you been thinking of proposing?"

Ambler failed to disclose that he still felt like he was married. Sacraments cannot be wholly taken back. They leave a mark - or wound. When he slept with anyone, he experienced a twinge, or more, of guilt. Perhaps he even felt more guilt now than he did when he was married.

"We're content at the moment. I worry that marriage could change that. You can still win if you stick, rather than twist," Marshal argued. He failed to disclose how much Grace wanted to get married - and have children. The hints she was making were more than just hints. They could eventually become an ultimatum. But Marshal would surrender to Grace. Marry her. He loved her. He would lose the battle but win the war.

Ambler half-listened to his friend, as the creeping barrage of his thoughts grew louder. The face he presented to Marshal and the world was as glib and insouciant as ever. But he subtly checked his phone a couple of times for a message from Birch. There was part of him which imagined that MI6 were tracking his phone and they would send a car to take him to a safehouse, in order to de-brief him. Time was supposed to be of the essence. Beneath the surface his nerves were a touch frayed, but for once Ambler felt purposeful. He was a second world war fighter pilot, who could die tomorrow. But he would still take to the skies if called upon, whether on Benzedrine or having taken a pill to cure him of the pox from a local girl - who had kissed other pilots goodbye as well.

He alternated between feeling queasy and emboldened. Ambler had spent enough time prevaricating. He now just wanted to get the operation over and done with. The decision was made. *Nothing is good or bad but thinking makes it so.* The life of a spy was one of secrets and lies. His existence so far, or certainly his married life, had been a dress rehearsal for the role.

Marshal got in some more drinks. Kitty almost pushed a colleague out of the way to serve him. The soldier would have probably flirted back with the barmaid in return in years gone by. Before Grace.

The two friends soon moved on to spirits and spoke about Hank Williams, the Third Crusade, Argentinian steak houses, Japanese whiskies and Graham Greene. The joe eventually forgot about hearing from his handler. "Soldiering is mostly about waiting around," Marshal had once declared. The spying game was similar.

The table of hedge fund managers grew more raucous. Their braying, plummy guffaws became no laughing matter. Ambler noticed how Marshal occasionally shot them a look like he wanted to kill them. Or at least maim one of the quartet. His features would momentarily harden, like a piece of clay being fired. Ambler had often wondered if the army had forged Marshal, or had it just given him a platform to be himself? But the former para merely simmered, instead of being brought to the boil. The enemy was as much of a source of amusement as anger. One didn't have to be a Marxist to be a useful or useless idiot - although it probably helped, Ambler half-drunkenly mused.

Marshal, whether drunk or sober, couldn't help but note how Ambler often appeared pre-occupied, whether drunk or sober. He had been even more distracted since leaving his ex-wife's house. Perhaps Sara had said something to him - or Ambler had failed to say something to her. Life is a patchwork of small and large regrets. Alternatively, it was not unheard of for an author to retreat into his own world. The writer may well have just been ruminating upon his latest novel. Marshal was not one to pry.

The soldier had his own species of a thousand-yard stare and was not immune to gazing out the window too. A lamplight flickered over a black Range Rover, replete with tinted glass, parked across the street from the pub. But Marshal had no cause to give the vehicle a second thought.

Inside the car, the brawny driver glared at Ambler with almost murderous intent - with piggy eyes. His tattooed hands gripped the steering wheel, his scarred knuckles as white as his shaven head. A tattoo of a couple of crossed hammers decorated his thick, shock-absorbing neck. His gnarled face appeared unamused and unimpressed. The thug wore a black suit, with a telescopic cosh tucked into the waistband. A half-smoked cigarette hung out the side of a cruel mouth. He had just sent a text message, updating his boss as to his location and the latest information on the author. The enforcer looked forward to confronting the writer in earnest. Punishing him. Tomorrow night would be the night.

8.

Mid-morning.

The sun screeched through a gap in the curtains and scolded Ambler, like a parent would a truant child. He felt too bleary-eyed and tired to even feel world-weary. His back was stiff, but back pain could no longer compete for space in the forefront of his mind. He checked his phone. There was a message from an old girlfriend, which he deleted, but no message from Birch. He craved a sense of urgency and importance, as if he had just entered a new religious order and wanted to prove himself. He was tempted to message Birch, but he didn't want to come across like a needy student pestering his tutor.

After gulping down the bottle of water by his bed and showering, Ambler glanced at the time and realised that he would be late for a meeting at his literary agency. Thankfully it was with Polly Fay, not Alexander Ponsonby, who looked after various ancillary rights. They were due to discuss an audio book strategy - or refine the one she came up with a year ago.

"Audio books are the future - and the future is now," the mumsnet.com subscriber had enthused. Enthusiasm had long trumped competence in the publishing industry. Ambler could remember how Polly had also said that interactive books, Netflix option rights, foreign sales, Apple, genre-busting novels and family sagas were the future. She had spoken passionately and seemingly intelligently about where she believed, or knew, the market was heading. Ambler thought how the world might be a better place if people cared less about things and admitted their ignorance.

The author messaged the agent to ask if he could push back the meeting. She promptly replied to say that she could meet at midday, but she was only in the office for a few hours as she had to attend her son's sports day. It seemed that the future could wait, if Ambler was unable to meet by one o'clock.

Marshal was waiting in the kitchen. He had drunk even more than Ambler last night but didn't seem to be feeling any ill effects. The sofa had been put back into order and the bedding neatly folded upon it. Marshal sat at the table with a cup of coffee, fifty or so pages into the copy of *Checkmate in Berlin* Ambler had bought him. The author had to admire his friend's constitution. He wondered if Marshal could outdrink him because the soldier had even more, graver sins to drown.

"Are we not due to be at your agency's offices this morning?" Marshal asked, after letting another brief nod serve as a greeting. It would remain unspoken in relation to whatever was said the previous evening. Wine truth isn't always full of verisimilitude.

"We are, but I postponed the meeting."

Ambler's phone vibrated and he reached for the device like a gunslinger reaching for his revolver. It was a text from Birch. The writer brought the phone up to his eyes and unblinkingly devoured the short message. Birch instructed Ambler to call him on an unfamiliar number at midday. He read the message over again and then sent a short email to Polly to apologise for having to now cancel their meeting. He couldn't be bothered to furnish her with an explanation.

"I'm going to have to cancel my appointment at the agency now," Ambler remarked to his friend, still half-distracted.

"All well?" Marshal replied, with a rare note of concern in his voice. The writer's features had dramatically altered when reading the message on his phone, as if Ambler had just heard from an embittered mistress, HMRC or an oncologist.

"Yes, it's nothing," the spy replied, lying. It felt like it was everything. "If you want to take half the day off. I suspect you need to relieve your dogsitter and catch-up with some things. I'll call you later as to the arrangements for the event this evening."

Ambler looked at his driver as he spoke to him, but his slightly haunted countenance suggested he was still staring at the message on his phone.

He answered the call. Birch spoke to him, the soul of formality. They were no longer old college friends, but joe and handler. Employer and employee. Ambler mused how Birch enjoyed acting as his superior a bit too much.

"I trust you are on your own? I have to ask. You are aware of some of our procedures, Daniel. You have researched and written about them. But you will not be familiar with all of them - and procedures are procedures. They exist to keep you - and us - safe. You will soon become a crew member on board our tight ship."

Ambler was sorely tempted to come out with a glib or sarcastic comment, but he remained silent. Even the office joker will behave himself on his first day. Birch informed Ambler as to the time and location of their meeting the following day.

"You will, of course, have questions. But I must ask you to make a mental note of such questions and present them tomorrow. You are an author, but from now on you must refrain from writing anything down in relation to the operation… I appreciate that you have already signed a version of the Official Secrets Act with us, but you will be asked to sign further documents tomorrow, covering additional security issues. One of our lawyers will be present to address any queries."

Ambler was on the cusp of replying that it seemed he was more likely to be wounded from a paper cut, rather than a Russian bullet, but desisted. The writer was used to signing contracts and NDAs. Again, Ambler thought how he had unwittingly been rehearsing for the role of a spy for half his life.

The author sat in his study after the call ended. He told himself that he should work to take his mind off things - but Ambler had little or no desire to work. Writing felt like frippery. He tried to read, but words felt stale. Unimportant. A strong wind might even blow them off the page. The literary editor had sent the copy of *Greene Land* via a courier. Without reading a single chapter of the book he knew how he would end the review, by recommending *Russian Roulette*, Richard Greene's recent biography of the novelist. He would be able to cobble together most of the copy by reading other reviews. He had done so before and would do so again. Ambler once had a dinner with several fellow authors. Someone asked the table how large a percentage of the book they read, when commissioned to write a review. The highest percentage was fifty.

How to kill time? Before time kills me.

Ambler looked up the flight times for Cuba. He then broke one of his golden rules by checking the rankings for some of his books on Amazon, scanning recent reader reviews as he did so. He was reminded why he set the rule not to do so in the first place. He made a cup of coffee, to help wake him up. But thought, as he finished the cup, how he wanted to fall asleep. Lunch was half-eaten, at best. He sent an email to the organiser of the event, which would take place later in the evening. Ambler was booked in to give a talk to *The Blackheath Writing Society*. He hoped that the talk might somehow be cancelled. He wanted the evening off, to prepare for his meeting the following day. Or get drunk. Or both. Ricky Nelson's *Garden Party* could be heard in the background:

"But if memories were all I sang

I'd rather drive a truck."

Some emails came in, but he ignored them. He drummed his fingers on his desk. He thought about updating his will. He played a couple of hands of online poker. Ambler had signed up to the site during his divorce, when he couldn't sleep. It had been six months since he had last logged-on. He was on edge.

Like Ricky Tar.

Ambler showed some willpower by not opening a bottle of wine, albeit he was far from proud or happy about the supposed display of character. Another day, another dolour. His mind prickled with questions - more questions than he possessed answers for. Could the entire operation be a stalking horse? The wily old KGB officer of Rybin could be bribing, blackmailing or threatening Vetrov to pass on false intelligence which might compromise the River House and embarrass them. Putin would revel in a small propaganda victory. Russia was obsessed with disseminating disinformation. It was like a Victorian parlour game to them, one played on an industrial level. They used more smoke and mirrors than a Las Vegas illusionist. Their aim could be to use the spy novelist as their joe, without Ambler knowing it. Had Birch and his office considered that Vetrov could be using the promise of treasure to compel the writer to visit him? Ambler recalled how his "friend" was fond of childish (sometimes cruel) pranks, and surprise parties. The eccentric oligarch, or former oligarch, might just be bored and want some company. He would be greeted with a bluff laugh and bear hug in Havana, rather than given any flash drive. Vetrov may be intending to make Ambler an offer he couldn't refuse, in relation to ghost writing his memoirs. Had Birch passed on knowledge of the operation to his counterparts in the US? The novelist had once written that "MI6 are the CIA's lapdog," much to the chagrin of a couple of UK intelligence officers he knew. Ambler might well be already working for some Republican hawk, rather than for Queen and country. How did they know that any compromising material couldn't be traced back to Vetrov - and Ambler? They could and should expect retaliation. It was doubtful that Rybin was the most forgiving of human beings. It was likely that the FSB still had kill teams in place. It had been a while since the Russians had assassinated anyone on UK soil, but that could just mean that they had acquired all their targets. They were just awaiting a new name. What security measures would be put in place, if the worst came to the worst? How trusted was Vetrov's intermediary? What would actually happen after he touched down in Cuba? Would it not appear suspicious if he only remained in the country for one or two days?

Ambler drank a second cup of coffee, whilst concluding that he should never have consumed the first. He needed some air. Or he needed to sleep.

It was now afternoon. His phone vibrated with a message. He thought it might be from Samantha. Should she be staying in a hotel close by he would visit her. Sex would distract him. But not for long, alas. But he would see her. Tick a box. But really Ambler wanted to see Sara again. The message, however, was from

Marshal. He was on his way. They would need to leave soon to drive across London to make the book talk in time.

Duty calls.

9.

White's.

The oldest and most exclusive gentleman's club in London. Established in the seventeenth century. "Stuffed with so much white privilege, people should be arrested just for being a member," one left-wing blogger commentated. The blogger was a member of *Soho House*, although his father had been a member of the *National Liberal Club*, because he had been unable to get into *White's*. *White's* was the king of clubs, or a club fit for a king. Prince Charles was a member. Prince William became a member shortly after his birth. Other members included David Cameron and Norman Lamont. The great and the good could rub shoulders with one another in its gilded, hallowed chambers, as well as venture capitalists and senior civil servants. Former army officers, who couldn't stomach each other when they served, could now sit down to an equitable lunch together. Noblemen would treat their accountants to a lavish supper as a thank you for helping them evade or avoid tax (the clients got confused about which) - and duly write off the bill as a business expense. Pension funds would be syphoned off over olives and a gin and tonic. The word "commoner" was still used, as liberally as the phrase "bloody foreigners". Or "my lawyer is sorting things".

Boyd Hamilton and Simon Birch sat in a couple of old but re-constituted wing-back chairs in a corner of the bar, out of earshot of others. They had just finished a lunch (the venison had been cooked to perfection, as members expected and demanded), and were now enjoying a glass or two of vintage port. The year was a good one, apparently.

"So, your man is in. Excellent. Good job," Boyd Hamilton remarked, in a voice even plummier than Birch's. Which was no mean feat. It would be "our man" if the operation proved a success. It would then be "my man" if Hamilton spoke to the Prime Minister, briefing him on the intelligence coup.

Boyd Hamilton. One day it would be "Sir" Boyd Hamilton, or his life would be deemed a failure. Educated at Winchester, Oxford and Sandhurst. Former officer in the Household Cavalry. Hamilton left the army because he felt he wasn't being "valued" and promoted with "sufficient alacrity" - and the second son received a "mere pittance" of an inheritance. Hamilton joined the Foreign Office and then MI6. He rose through the ranks and made a name for himself, like Napoleon. Or one of Napoleon's less accomplished brothers. The ambitious department head spent a great deal of time with various media liaison officers, ensuring that he controlled any narratives. He was often out to lunch or dinner with the right minister, mandarin, diplomat or opposite number from across the pond. But "that was the job", he explained, with a sigh that wasn't altogether sincere. The head of the Russia desk knew how to flatter his paymasters in Whitehall - or paint such worrying scenarios that budget increases were assured, even if cutbacks had to be made elsewhere. "We are the first and last line of defence," Hamilton would firmly state, believing his words too, to the latest insipid bureaucrat who held the purse strings.

Mid-fifties. Elegantly attired. Mildly handsome. Mildly distinguished looking. Tall and thin, like Anthony Blunt. Boyd Hamilton still exhibited the remnants of a military background in his bearing and gait. He had a narrow, varnished countenance which could appear charming when called upon. It was likely that the ex-cavalry officer dyed his hair, and even likelier he owned a sunbed. Birch fancied that his boss resembled a Victorian gentleman - or villain. Had he lived in the nineteenth century, Hamilton would have been high-up in the East India Company - embezzling funds, whilst appearing a paragon of probity.

"Did you do as advised and persuade him that he could become the hero in his own story?" he added, partly to accrue some of the credit for recruiting their new agent.

"I told him what he wanted to hear. He will be a slightly reluctant hero, but a hero nevertheless," Birch replied, taking a sip of port and glancing around the bar. He couldn't see any skirt or smell any perfume, unfortunately. The air smelled of furniture polish and lamb cutlets. The lamb was tender of course, so those with dentures could work their way through any dish.

"I haven't read any of his novels, of course, but I know the type. There are joes who we can coerce through blackmail and threats. Then there are those who will sell out their country, or own mother, for thirty pieces of silver. But some we may deem crusaders still, rather than capitalists. Idealogues and zealots. Heroes or fools. At least you will not have to go through any unpleasantness of coercing or threatening an old friend. I hope he harboured some doubts, however. Otherwise, I might be suspicious. We do not want an over-keen or reckless volunteer. We have also done our due diligence, despite or because of his connection to you? We usually say trust but verify. When it comes to anything to do with our Russian friends, however, the mantra must be distrust and verify. We have been burned before by Trojan horses. We should not believe that we have found a unicorn, just because we want to believe it. I would prefer not to clasp a snake to my bosom. Have we double-checked the financials? Our joe hasn't recently come into any money, courtesy of Moscow or anywhere else? The fellow is recently divorced. Ex-wives and lawyers are unforgiving creatures. He has also been paying for medical care for a recent back injury. He lives in Kensington. I dare say he doesn't want to use the NHS, like a commoner. He didn't yearn to go to Cambridge, rather than Oxford, in his youth - and pin posters of Burgess and Philby on his bedroom wall? You could say that our chap attended all the right schools, but through bursaries and scholarships. History teaches us that the right schools can be the wrong schools too. There is no chance that our joe could be their joe? It is my job to ask - and re-ask."

It was here that Hamilton thought how he wished he possessed the resources of his American counterparts. Man for man he would back the quality of the personnel fighting under his banner, but God is on the side of the big battalions. He had too short a time, with too few personnel, to run a deep dive on everything.

Hamilton was tempted to let the Americans in on the operation, but they would soon take over and side-line him. The big beast would be made to feel small. No, Vetrov would be his asset. Treasure chest. His department also now controlled the key, in Ambler. They deserved the win. *I deserve the win.* But what would the key ultimately open the door to? Hamilton had been kept awake of late, imagining reading headlines about a disgraced Russian minister, an embarrassment to Putin and his regime. Or Rybin could be turned. "Rasputin" could become the new Oleg Gordievsky. The wily old Russian fox could become as meek as a lamb. A lamb to the slaughter. If ever Keith Jeffery wrote an addendum to his history of MI6, Hamilton would be included (anonymously or otherwise) in its pages. The operation could secure his seat in the House of Lords. Hamilton could be forgiven for thinking how he could purchase his dream holiday home, just outside of Lisbon. He could find some peace and quiet away from his wife - and gain the attention of his mistress.

"His financials are clean. He earns far more than the average author - and his wife was kind enough not to castrate him in the divorce settlement. His relationship with Vetrov is genuine," Birch replied, calmly re-answering any questions that his superior was re-asking. "I have known Daniel for longer than I have known my wife. I dare say I also trust him more than her too."

"The file said that our man drinks a lot," Hamilton stated, after finishing off another glass of port.

"What joe doesn't drink a lot?" Birch replied, half wanting to add that he hadn't met a wholly sober handler either. "But that doesn't mean that he drinks too much. It's unlikely that Vetrov would invite our man to stay if he was a teetotaller."

"Indeed. We will not need to coach Ambler in how to break black bread or drink vodka. But we will need to brief him on other things, once we get his signature on the dotted line. No matter how much research our spy novelist has done, he will need some basic training," Hamilton remarked, before suddenly holding up his hand, akin to a Nazi salute, to indicate to an approaching waiter that they did not want to be disturbed. Spying was secrecy.

Loose lips sink ships. He hoped that the staff knew who he was, the position he held. Most of the waitering staff knew the self-important member as the diner who liked to claim that the wine was corked, pretending to be an expert. "Take Tanner with you tomorrow. He will know how to instil a bit of loyalty and fear into our joe, as well as train him. Keep reassuring our man too, if needs be. The novelist may be prone to bouts of paranoia, as well as flights of fancy. We need to get him on that plane and into that villa, as soon as humanly or inhumanly possible. Our emissary will be in touch soon as to when he expects our carrier pigeon will arrive. It seems that both parties are keen to conclude this business quickly, which alarms and fortifies me in equal measure. We cannot afford any mistakes. *You* cannot afford any mistakes, Simon. I need everyone's A-game."

Birch nodded, appearing as grave as grave could be. It was left unsaid that his boss would not think twice in scapegoating his subordinate should the operation blow up in their faces - or become a damp squib. It was also surely implicit that Birch would not think twice in scapegoating his old friend from university, if he needed to save his own skin. Despite all the chatter, wealth of files and debriefings most things remained unsaid in the intelligence community. It was a world of secrets and lies. Like a marriage.

Boyd Hamilton offered up a disapproving look as a couple of younger members (forty plus years of age) laughed a little too loudly, whilst sitting at the bar. Life may have been lots of things to the head of the Russia desk, but it certainly wasn't amusing.

Birch covertly glanced at his watch. He was keen to wrap things up. He had a date with his lawyer's secretary later in the evening. He also needed to do some work to prepare for the operation. Birch could only stay and appear grateful for his superior's pearls of wisdom for so long. He needed time to go home and change, dress younger for the twenty-something secretary. But duty called. Despite his desire to leave, Birch still needed to discuss a tidbit of information which, if he didn't mention it, could come back to bite him on the arse.

DUTY CALLS

A report had come across his desk that morning, citing that Sergei Shunin had re-entered the country. Shunin was an agent in the FSB, responsible for leading kill squads. The bald-headed agent had two confirmed kills on British soil. Both had been former Russian operatives who had defected. Shunin had poisoned the first. The second had been made to appear like a mugging, which had turned into a murder. Confirmed kills may have been just two, but Shunin was suspected of being involved in over a dozen assassinations (including the deaths of money launderers, less than judicious lawyers, senior gangland bosses and a Ukrainian journalist). The report had included a grainy photograph from a traffic camera of the piggy-eyed former soldier, as he sat in the back of a black Range Rover (with false number plates).

10.

Although Ambler was far from enamoured with the areas of New Cross and Deptford, he always liked driving up the hill and encountering the wide-open space and greenery of Blackheath. Whether the air felt fresher or not, it seemed fresher. It was like another realm, separate from the rest of London. A village. He could believe that the world wasn't all that bad (just sometimes ghastly, like people). The light was fading, but not melancholy. A few kites, flown by fathers and sons, kept striving upwards. A few families still congregated on the lush grass. All manner of dogs darted about, playing with old friends and new. Sun-kissed women in summer dresses read trashy paperbacks. A few students drank lager from cans and played frisbee, unfortunately.

The writer was due to give a talk to *The Blackheath Writing Society*. He had done so for the past five years, a legacy or hangover from living in Greenwich. Sara had originally contacted them to propose that "the local author" meet the group. She always supported his career far more than he did hers. It was another thing which Ambler felt guilty about, but it needed to get in line, like a child due to take communion on a Sunday. There were plenty of other sins to dwell on. During the first year of living in Greenwich, Ambler had crested the hill, itching to see Sara. To make love to her. But, eventually, on more than one occasion Ambler had driven up the hill whilst checking for any vestiges of lipstick on his mouth or collar, returning home from a night away with a mistress - having told Sara that he had attended a speaking engagement. He would keep one hand on the wheel whilst spraying himself with deodorant to mask the smell of perfume.

Marshal noted how distracted Ambler was. It wasn't due to any stage fright. His passenger kept checking his phone, expecting an important message. Maybe he was waiting on news about a book deal, or a woman was due to text. The soldier smiled to himself, as he thought of Grace and realised how happy he was to be out of the dating game.

The Blackheath Community Hall was just as Ambler remembered it, alackaday. Polished wooden floors. A faint smell of bleach and lavender, which wasn't faint enough. The window next to the door was decorated with posters, advertising various events and associations. *The Blackheath Bridge Group*, *The Blackheath* and *Greenwich Local History Society* and *The Blackheath Sudoku and Backgammon Ass* were due to meet within the coming month. A local school was putting on a production of *The Railway Children*. A "Non-Binary Life Coach", whoever or whatever that was, was giving a talk to the local Liberal Democrat Association. "All pronouns" were welcome.

Marshal had made a tactical retreat, agreeing to pop by towards the end of the event after having a pint at the local pub. He left the Jag in the back corner of the nearby carpark, which was surprisingly devoid of other vehicles.

Ambler was greeted by Gordon Turner. The sixty-year-old widower was the chairperson of the writing group, having changed his title from chairman a couple of years ago, after reading an article in *The Independent*. Turner was wearing his customary faded beige suit, with mud-brown elbow patches and an ink-stain on the breast pocket. The retired civil servant was also the chairperson of the local bridge and history societies, as well as the leader of the local Scout group. He looked slightly older than he was, like a worn coin that should perhaps come out of circulation. Yet he duly beamed at his guest speaker.

"Evening, Daniel," Turner announced, striding towards him and shaking the novelist's hand a little too vigorously for a little too long. For the first two visits the chairperson had formally called him "Mr Ambler". The author then insisted that he be called "Daniel". In some ways, Ambler regretted the decision. Turner sounded like an extra from *The Archers*, or the lead in a small amateur dramatic society. Turner was uncommonly cheerful and selfless. Sweet-natured. Initially, Ambler believed that the man involved himself in his local community due to feeling lonely, or the civil servant still craved a modicum of bureaucratic power. But he realised he had been uncharitable in such thoughts. The widower, who still missed his late wife, was one of the more genuinely decent people that Ambler knew.

"Are you well?" Turner added.

"Well enough," Ambler replied, with a just about convincing enough polite smile. Spying is acting.

"You will see some old faces and new ones this evening, as usual. If you can allow plenty of time at the end for questions. You know how we like to quiz you. Now, would you like some tea, coffee or a glass of wine? Let me get you something."

"That's very kind, but you probably have half a dozen things and people to attend to. I can help myself, thank you."

Ambler made his way over to a couple of trestle tables where some refreshments were laid out. Homemade Victoria sponges, carrot cakes and apple tarts. Sausage rolls, which looked dryer than the author's wit, along with cheeses and pickled onions, graced the tables. Tea, coffee, orange squash and some intolerable wine. Ambler poured himself a glass of the latter, as he surveyed the scene.

Thirty to fifty souls were expected. The author had spoken to larger audiences, but he had also given talks to smaller groups. He wasn't (too) proud. Quite a few people were already filing in, wittering to one another. Some covertly glanced at him, as if he were a local movie star. A handful carried folders with them. Clutching them. Lovingly. Ambler dearly hoped that no one would try to pass on a manuscript for him to read or hand on to his agent. There was a time when the writer had generously let his readers thrust their typed manuscripts or flash drives into his hands, gifting them the hope that he would read their work and recommend them to his agent and publisher. He was kinder back then. When he was faithful. Happily married to Sara. Perhaps those things were linked. He could count the number of people under forty on one hand. Many wore their best floral dresses and had slapped on some make-up, as if they were attending church on a Sunday. Most were pleasant looking. A smattering seemed haughty. Some were fans of Somerset Maughan, Anthony Trollope and Penelope Lively. Each to their own. Ambler fancied how he had almost stepped back in time. They probably thought how Ted Heath, or Clement Attlee even, was still Prime Minister. There were worse eras to live in, however.

A few familiar faces came into view, of course. There was Margaret Chard, a plump, bustling ex-accountant with an aggressive perm and shrill manner. Margaret had been working on a memoir of her late father, Percival Chard, for the past five years. She also wrote cosy crime fiction, centred around a retired accountant who worked at a cat sanctuary. The first three (self-published) titles in the series were *A Purrfect Crime, Paws For Thought and Claws In The Contract.* Margaret would doubtlessly - depressingly - corner Ambler and update him on how the series was progressing at some point during the evening. Brian Teller, a retired policeman who spent half the year in his villa in Malaga (living a stone's throw away from the villains he once investigated), was also duly in attendance. Teller was standing ramrod straight with his back to the wall, wearing a freshly dry-cleaned suit and Hush Puppies, twiddling the ends of his battleship-grey moustache. He narrowed his eyes and scrutinised everyone who strolled through the door, as if they were suspects in an ongoing investigation. He wrote police procedural crime. "I'm a professional. I've lived it. Other people just write about it." Ambler couldn't speak to the quality of the writing, but his covers and blurbs were decidedly amateurish. Teller reminded Ambler of the Major from Fawlty Towers. The policeman was mildly racist and more than slightly sexist - but basically decent and harmless.

Ambler observed how Teller stared at one of his fellow society members with a strange mixture of lust, frustration and disapproval. Cindy Weaver had arrived on the scene, drawing everyone's attention like moths to a flame. Cindy was the queen, princess or glamour-puss of the writing group. Of course, other women envied and disliked her, behind a façade of suburban

71

civility. Not only was the wealthy divorcee uncommonly attractive, but she had also committed the cardinal sin of being successful. Her novel, *A Cornish Affair*, had been published by a small, independent press. The local newspaper ran a profile piece, on page four no less. The book cover was placed at a jaunty angle, next to a photograph of the author, who was glowing from a tan and sense of fulfilment. Cindy had big hair, a small waist and a surgically enhanced bosom. It was arguable that the ageing divorcee, whose partners got younger, was past her prime. But the woman had an attractive attitude, that the best was yet to come. A decade of smoking in her twenties had furnished her voice with an alluring huskiness. Ambler imagined that Cindy could secure voiceover jobs, for *Waitrose* or *Dairy Milk,* if she wanted to. But Cindy had no need or desire to work. She married - and divorced - well. Ambler had accepted the brazen woman's invitation to have dinner a year or so ago, ostensibly to advise on her latest manuscript. He was tempted to sleep with her, just to make his ex-wife jealous. The salacious gossip would have reached Sara's ears, passing from Blackheath into neighbouring Greenwich, within a month. There was sufficient cruelty in the world without the novelist needing to add to the surplus, however. He merely kissed her on the cheek after dinner, when she leaned in to say goodnight. Cindy stood out, especially in *The Blackheath Writing Society*. A peacock among pigeons. The tallest poppy. She wore a tight-fitting couture dress, which flaunted her figure, and designer kitten heels. Ambler fancied that Cindy quite enjoyed being the centre of attention - and being envied and disliked by her supposed friends. It amused her. Her crimson lips sculptured themselves into a self-satisfied smile, every time that the likes of Margaret Chard offered up a puritanical frown to the "hussy".

The would-be writers also stared at the bestselling novelist. Starry-eyed. Ambler was an embodiment of their hopes and dreams. They too might one day be published by Penguin or the like, give interviews, feature in the bestseller charts, have a well-known actor read their audiobook, be asked to sign a new hardback for an adoring fan. If they could just have an agent or publisher read their work and recognise its potential.

Ambler did his bit to feign interest and politely answer questions when he was approached by a few members. At least they distracted him from the taste of the wine. They spoke about their "WIP" - and how beta readers had loved the latest draft of their manuscript. Ambler was asked if he could recommend a top editor, who would charge a reasonable fee, to help polish up a dystopian eco-thriller. How many twitter followers did a writer need to be judged successful? Somebody had to be the next E.L James, why couldn't it be them? Did the author know anyone in the film industry who they could send their novel to? A beta reader said that their YA novella, about a three-legged dragon, would make a great film. It was less of a literary matter, of course, but Margaret Chard asked if it was best to make quince or jam with her apricots. Whether they were being genuine or not, most of the members who spoke to Ambler topped or tailed their conversation by telling him how much they enjoyed his books. There were worse miseries to endure, he mused, than adulation.

Tonight was the night.

The wide tires of the Range Rover crunched upon some stray gravel, which had scattered across the asphalt from the path which ran around the carpark. The three letters on the number plate on the black SUV were the same as the initials of the author giving a talk in the nearby community hall. The gnarled-looking driver of the vehicle now had three passengers. Two fellow enforcers. One boss. The latter's face appeared the hardest and cruellest, however. The tip of his index finger tapped away upon his knee, as if sending a message in Morse code. He was eager to take care of business. The carpark was thankfully deserted. The driver of the Jaguar was absent. There were no CCTV cameras surveilling the immediate area. A line of leafy elm trees prevented prying eyes in the close by terrace houses from witnessing anything. The driver of the Range Rover parked not too far away and not too close to the Jaguar. Not all the surrounding street lamps were working. Clouds snuffed out the moon and stars. They would do what they had to do in the half-light. The night would swallow up their crimes. It was as if God was on their side.

11.

It dawned on Ambler, around two years ago, that he still preferred talking about his earlier work than he did his spy novels. The present day seemed dull and uninspiring, compared to the past. If he could somehow encourage a dozen people to read Pushkin and Chekhov, then his life might finally be a tiny bit worthwhile.

Ambler stood at a lectern with a drink to hand. He appeared far too carefree and content to be mistaken for a priest in a pulpit. Thankfully, someone had turned his acidic wine into water. Cindy Weaver sat at the front, crossing and flashing her tanned legs a couple of times when the speaker looked her way. The gesture amused rather than distracted him. Cindy flashed her smile too, which revealed a piece of chocolate cake in between her otherwise gleaming teeth. Margaret Chard took copious notes, as though the writer were a chef revealing the recipe for his secret sauce. A couple of gummy spinsters sat at the back, looking so alike as to seem like sisters, and caught up on their knitting. They may have just wandered in by accident, Ambler fancied. He took a sip of water, to prevent himself from laughing. Being an author isn't all glamour.

He spoke for approximately thirty minutes about his latest novel, treading the well-rehearsed line between telling the story whilst not giving too much away. The audience appeared engaged, but he started to bore himself. Ambler had offered up his spiel countless times before, like a singer trotting out his only hit.

"Any questions?" he asked. In a similar way to how Ambler had just feigned enthusiasm for what he was saying, he now pretended to be interested in his readers, as he suppressed another yawn. He wished someone could turn his water into wine once more, or something stronger.

One hand immediately shot up, as if punching the air with glee. Ambler had learned to distrust those who champed at the bit to ask the first question. They usually liked the sound of their own voice, even more than the speaker, or had a political agenda. Ambler remembered the sallow faced man who put his hand up from the previous year. He was wearing the same moth-eaten cardigan, although the badges emblazoned with the latest left-wing political slogans were different. His name was Lionel Cromwell. Last year he had asked if the security services had ever considered Jeremy Corbyn an intelligence threat, although the preamble to his question was tantamount to a party-political broadcast.

"Corbyn may well be a threat to intelligence. Or, having heard his policies, intelligence may be the last thing I would associate with the man," Ambler drily joked, although a fifth of the audience demurred from joining in the laughter. Lionel emitted a scowl, as if sucking upon two lemons. Perhaps the peace-loving socialist was close to writing the author's name down in a black book, so he would face a reckoning at a later date.

Out of mild spite, or to save the audience from a pontificating lecture, Ambler pretended not to see the raised hand and pointed to a woman on the other side of the room, who wanted to ask a question.

"I read in your bio that you attended Oxford and studied Russian. Were you ever approached to join MI6?"

"My father was a humble postman. MI6 are keen on recruiting from much grander stock. Perhaps they also realised how much of a physical and moral coward I am," Ambler half-jested. "I'm afraid that not even the Scrabble Society asked me to join their ranks during my university days. Quite rightly, I might add."

The audience laughed. The sound was a more welcome tonic than alcohol, or at least equal to it.

The next question came from Trevor Waring, a former history teacher who devoutly read - and re-read - Eric Hobsbawm. Waring had faced several rejection letters for his "literary" thrillers, each approximately two hundred thousand words long.

He still believed that he just needed to get one of his manuscripts into the hands of the right agent at the right time to succeed (as his books touched on pressing social issues). Waring had been writing now for ten years, but he still steadfastly refused to self-publish. Turner mentioned to Ambler how the former teacher spent most of his time critiquing the works of his fellow members.

"Mr Ambler, you cited in your talk that Russia is both the old and new enemy. Are you saying that we are embarking upon a new cold war? Also, isn't it all so subjective? The two sides - the east and west, capitalism and communism - both have as much blood on their hands as the other. Also, can it not be argued too that spies can be the cause of problems, rather than the solution to them?"

His voice was reedy, his chin as pointed as Jimmy Hill's and, behind thick tortoiseshell glasses, he seemed to permanently squint.

"I'm not entirely sure that the previous cold war ever ended. For the KGB turned FSB, I dare say it didn't. As for the west having as much blood on its hands as certain communist regimes, there are several million kulaks, starved Chinese people, denounced and executed dissidents, murdered Uighurs and others who may beg to differ. I may be being unfashionable, but there is still something to be said for democracy - and even capitalism. As Churchill said, "Democracy is the worst form of government, except for all the others." As to whether spies can be the cause of problems, I agree with you. But mostly they are responsible for marital and drinking problems."

Less audience laughter.

Justin Ford, a merchant banker who had the misfortune of growing up in Los Angeles, asked the next question. Ford had installed an expensive shepherd hut in his garden a few months ago, in order to have "a special place" to write. The American had taken plenty of photographs of the hut and written a blog about it but had still only written three pages of his latest manuscript.

"You are known for killing off your main characters and leaving your readers with a sense of melancholy at the end. Do you think that's always wise?"

"I'm not sure if it's wise or not, but if you are searching for a happy ending you may want to read a fairy tale or see a movie. Nobody gets out of this world alive, I'm afraid. I'd be tempted to keep my characters alive, of course, if the publishers offered the right advance for a sequel."

Ambler carried on, making sure to repeat the questions so those in the group who were hard of hearing could follow things:

"What's the most important thing that a writer can do? The answer is read. Read Tolstoy, read Shakespeare, read Agatha Christie, read Dickens, read Cicero, read Chekhov, read Austen, read Greene, read Dostoyevsky. If you are interested in writing spy fiction, read le Carré, Alan Judd, Henry Porter and the like. It will be very difficult for you to write in any great tradition, if you are unaware what that tradition entails… How much money do I earn from each book? Myself and my accountant might say not enough. My fellow authors, who earn less, might argue too much."

Towards the end of the hour Ambler noticed Marshal come in quietly and sit at the back. Nobody gave him a second look, aside from Cindy Weaver. Initially the author thought about how he would grab a beer and curry with his driver. He needed a proper drink too, to wash the taste of the wine out his mouth. It was important to remember to forget. Ambler was checked in his desire to get drunk again. He needed to be up early tomorrow and at his best. To impress his new employer. A good night's sleep was called for, albeit he feared it may prove more elusive than the fifth man. Ambler thought how he might like to accept one of the manuscripts the group would offer and read it as he climbed into bed. It could prove more effective than Valium.

Time was up, thankfully. The applause was more than solely polite. Just about. Ambler signed a few books. He was always pleased to see tattered - used - paperbacks. A smattering of people tried to hand him their manuscript to read. Ambler apologised and explained that he was going out to dinner after the event and did not want to risk losing their work. It would be best if they could email him, via Gordon. He would then get back to them if he could help in any way.

Ambler craved a drink. The author couldn't help but observe how the usually stoical Marshal looked as bored as Ambler felt. He was soon cornered by Brian Teller, wanting to put the world, or something more important, to rights as he devoured his second custard cream biscuit.

"Spooks! They always acted so mysteriously when we had dealings with them, as though they were the only ones on the room who knew what was going on. But they were just as much in the dark as the rest of us. Only the villains have a plan and know what is going to happen. Never trust a spook is what I say. Better still, never put yourself into a position where you need to trust one."

The spy novelist was only half-listening to the former policeman, though. Distracted as he was by Cindy Weaver, pouting and offering up a suggestive smile across the crowded room. Ambler didn't know whether to laugh or reciprocate. He thought how Samantha would have looked good in the dress she was wearing too.

"You were entertaining and informative, as always, Daniel," Gordon Turner cordially remarked, after he signed the last book and rebuffed the last person to offer him their latest manuscript. "Thank you. You have given our members much to think about, no? We will keep scribbling away, cutting out the excess adjectives, and using fewer exclamation marks!"

"Yes," Ambler replied, humouring the man, as he thought of the Christopher Hitchens quote once more. *"Everyone has a book in them, but in most cases that is where it should stay."*

"My late wife, Pamela, would have greatly enjoyed your talk. She always meant to get around to writing a book. She was forever reading," Turner said, his voice close to breaking. The widower placed a finger beneath his glasses and wiped his eye. His face suddenly and briefly scrunched up, as if he had just bitten on a particularly hot chilli. Ambler thought how if Sara was present, she would have felt a wave of compassion and known exactly what to say. He felt a surplus of awkwardness and wished for Marshal to come over and save him. If the moment called for a glib comment Ambler could have helped. But it didn't. He regretted not working out a signal with his driver beforehand, for when he wanted to leave.

The chairperson eventually apologised and regained his composure. The guest speaker replied, courteously but somewhat hollowly, that there was nothing to apologise for.

"Same time again, next year?" Turner said, as the two men shook hands and parted. In the background, cakes were being wrapped in foil, teacups carefully placed back into cupboards and blue tack removed from A4 posters promoting the event.

"Why not?" the author answered. If given time, however, Ambler could probably think of a list of five reasons why he should decline the invitation.

12.

The temperature dropped. The air grew gloomier, like the world had been dipped in ink. The attractive town houses appeared a little gothic. The two men walked back to the car. Marshal hoped there wouldn't be too much traffic. He wanted to get home to Violet. Blackheath was far from a hive of activity, but a few people were out for the evening, in "the village" as the residents said with some snobbish pride. They didn't take kindly to being informed that their village was less than a mile away from Deptford and Lewisham. An ambulance sounded in the background. Ambler was reminded of his accident - and then reminded of his back pain. Like guilt, it only hurt when he thought about it. The solution of course was not to think about it. *Nothing is good or bad but thinking makes it so.*

Ambler sighed, but not wholly wearily. Part of him, enough of him, had enjoyed the event. Some of the questions amused him, or he amused the audience with his answers. Laughter is the best medicine. A few people also seemed to take his advice on board. If he could help just one would-be writer improve or finish their novel, then he had done his job. The event had also distracted him from his now other job. Every third thought, hammering on his frontal lobe like a blacksmith, had concerned Rybin, Vetrov and the proposed operation. There were more questions and fewer answers.

Again, Ambler was tempted to confide in his friend. He trusted Marshal, far more than he trusted Birch, he realised. From a certain point of view, he was about to be posted overseas and sent into battle. A problem shared is never a problem halved, but Ambler would value Marshal's opinion. But, again, he desisted. Stepped back from the ledge. Spying is secrecy. Spying is distrust. The chances of him being under surveillance were slim, but real. What if they had bugged his house or even Marshal's car? What if they put him through a polygraph tomorrow and asked if he had divulged any details of the operation to anyone? Spying is paranoia. He could be dismissed, or charged with treason, on his first day, if he was found to be a leaky ship. He could be excommunicated before even being baptised, the lapsed Catholic thought. It would not be the most glorious start to a career in the intelligence service, but it might still be more glorious than some.

An eerie atmosphere descended, dropping like the temperature. Something felt amiss, even before Ambler realised things were amiss. The carpark, as dark as a fresh bruise, was deserted - aside from Marshal's car at the rear and a black Range Rover. Containing four, spectral passengers. Only the light of a phone screen lit up the interior. Maybe the four men were just waiting for someone - and they would then set-off. They could just be listening to a football match on the radio. Taking coke. Surely they couldn't have been watchers from MI6, dispatched to keep an eye on their new asset? Even the clumsiest of operatives would prove subtler, Ambler judged.

Marshal's eyes narrowed, his features hardened (even more) - as if his alert level had altered and he was about to move to an equivalent of *Defcon 4*.

The evening breeze ran through a line of nearby trees, halfway between a hissing and shushing noise, kicking up an empty crisp packet.

The doors to the Range Rover opened, almost in unison. The light inside the car automatically came on. The spectral figures became all too real. Four suits. Four pairs of polished shoes. Four open collared, reasonably ironed shirts. Two gold chains. Three close shaven heads. All white. One Slavic looking. Six large fists, like mace-heads hanging off their long arms. One boss. One purpose. Six fists became five as the driver retrieved a black, telescopic steel baton from his pocket.

A chill ran down Ambler's injured back. His heart rate increased - moving from a trot, to a canter and then a gallop in a London minute. He felt nauseated, like someone had just told him he had stage four, terminal, liver cancer. The colour drained from his face, like water swirling down a plughole. He began to fear the worst. To dread. There was no hard evidence at present to think that the four men were here for him. That they were Russians. A kill squad. He just started to believe or know it. A wiser man might have fled there and then. Spying is paranoia. Just because you're paranoid, it doesn't mean that people are not out to get you. But perhaps the novelist needed to see the scene playout. Perhaps he was frozen to the spot. It would have been ignominious, to say the least, to abandon his friend too. Or perhaps they were already past the point of no return. They had walked beyond the Range Rover and were closer to Marshal's Jag. Should Ambler attempt to run back towards the entrance to the carpark he could be easily cut off. Even if he ran, he felt like his legs would give way.

"We run a tight ship," Ambler recalled Birch saying. The Titanic could be a less leaky ship. Spying is deception. Spying is fighting a losing battle. Birch had also mentioned that the novelist was about to become part of the new "great game". But it seemed like the game might already be up for him.

The eerie atmosphere morphed into a menacing one.

Marshal instinctively moved in front of his friend and client. His pulse remained remarkably even. One of the things that the paratrooper took away from his regiment was its motto: *Ready for Anything*. He quickly but methodically took in the approaching quartet, scanning for any telling bulges in pockets. If they were professional hitmen, it was likely that their targets would be dead by now. Or they would be dead very soon, at the very least. Ambler didn't seem to recognise them. His fans probably carried hardbacks of his books rather than extendable coshes. Marshal had made enemies of both the Albanian mafia and IRA in the past year or so, but he believed he was a ghost to them. Although maybe they were about to make a ghost out of him. The soldier surmised that, at best, the men in front of him were semi-professionals. But you never knew. It was four against two. Or more likely it would be three against one. Marshal wasn't expecting much from their boss, or his own.

Shock and fear were chiselled into Ambler's expression, like words carved into a gravestone. Thankfully, the author had gone to the toilet before leaving the venue, otherwise he would have relieved himself now. Ambler thought of Sara, rather than Samantha. He felt guilty that he had unwittingly condemned his friend. Even if he had the time for a garbled, babbling explanation to Marshal, he probably wouldn't have believed him. There would be no reasoning or negotiating with the figures in front of them. Kill squads were not known for their compassion.

The black-haired boss, a Rolex flashing beneath the sleeve of his suit jacket, walked at the head of the group - but not too far ahead. Marshal calmly took him in. Mid-forties. Medium build. Diamond stud in his ear. Capped teeth. Botoxed brow. Skin stretched across his face, reptilian-like. Slender nose, like a shark's fin. Petty, vicious eyes.

"Thou shalt not covet thy neighbour's wife," Connor Mason flatly, rather than playfully, stated with a pronounced sneer. The small-time gangster would enjoy turning his grievance into vengeance. After dishing out a beating to the writer that he would never forget, Mason would then turn his attention to his wife, Veronica. *The bitch*. Beat her. Divorce her. Leave her with nothing but regret. Thankfully he didn't have any children with his third wife.

Ambler's look of petrification was nudged towards one of confusion. Perhaps it was because he was expecting a Russian accent, as opposed to a London one.

Mason addressed his soon to be victim when he spoke. He possessed little or no concern for the driver - although Darren, his own driver, eyed his opposite number with more than a slither of antagonism.

Connor Mason. Half-Jewish, half-Irish. It was difficult to know which half was better or worse. His father had been a Hatton Garden diamond merchant, who fenced stolen gems and helped launder money for various criminal gangs. The son, after coming of age, having attended the best private schools that money could buy and been introduced to his father's business associates, opened a couple of nightclubs - selling drugs and laundering money through the "high-class" establishments. Mason fell in with more of the wrong, or right, kind of people. His empire grew. So did his ego. Occasionally disputes escalated and needed to be settled, although the asthmatic preferred not to get blood on his own hands, employing others to do his bidding. Married three times. No children (the rumour was that the gangster fired blanks, but no one was brave or stupid enough to discuss the issue with the boss). Despite openly having a string of mistresses - and sometimes housing them in the bungalow by his pool at his home in Chislehurst, Mason was understandably upset when he discovered that his wife was conducting an affair from reading a series of messages on her phone. He knew his name was Daniel. He knew he was a writer. The bitch had mentioned one of his books in her texts and so he found out his surname and what he looked like from his website. He knew they had spent one, or more, nights together. He knew that the writer was due to have lunch at the *Skylon* restaurant. Mason sent his men to follow Ambler and find out where he lived. The writer's website also furnished the wronged husband with his event schedule. Tonight was the night. The carpark was the first location they tried, in relation to tracking down the Jag. They just had to wait. Mason would treat the writer like anyone else who had disrespected him, as if he had dishonoured a debt or stolen from him. The gangster would beat respect into him.

"I don't want to hear if the bitch told you that she wasn't married," Mason added, adjusting his cufflinks. "Women lie, it's what they do. Most of the time they lie to themselves. You just need to take your medicine now. Veronica will have to do the same."

Mason thought how he would first allow his men to have their fun. The boss would get his kicks too, quite literally, once his victim was helpless, curled up in a ball, crying, on the ground. The writer's punishment would be severe, but not too severe. It would be commensurate with the crime. If he cracked a rib or lost a tooth, then so be in. He would be wise not to go to the hospital, or police. Mason could easily arrange an alibi. He had done so for before and he would doubtless do so again. No, it wouldn't go well for his victim if he tried to run to the police or retaliate. Seek justice.

When he heard Veronica's name then things started to slot into place for Ambler. Strangely, he felt more relief than fear when he realised that he was about to suffer a beating. His heartbeat slowed. The author was still lost for words, however.

Marshal took in the three enforcers, after surveying their employer. The thug closest to him, carrying his now extended baton, would be the one to attack first. *Baton Boy*, Marshal christened him. He was built powerfully enough, albeit the middle-aged man was now more flab than muscle. As loyal and as vicious as a mastiff. He was either a bouncer or ex-bouncer, Marshal surmised. He couldn't help but notice the West Ham "Hammers" tattoo on his neck.

Behind *Baton Boy*, breathing heavily, as if he might even be snoring, stood an even older and stouter figure. Patrick Duggan. Hungry, Duggan started to chew the inside of his mouth. He looked like a masticating bulldog. The fifty-year old had served as muscle for Mason's father, as a young man. He helped debt-collect and punish those who fell behind on their payments. Duggan had round shoulders and a rounder face. A bulbous, red nose, clown-like, squatted upon the middle of his countenance. Patrick Duggan liked to drink. He liked to hurt people too. He always liked it when certain patrons - the blacks and the queers - made trouble when he refused them entry into the nightclub that he worked the door of. The bull of a man appeared intimidating, but not to Marshal.

The last man, Liam Quinn (or "Paddypower" as he was nicknamed), was younger and slimmer - but cut from the same cloth as his colleagues. Hard-faced and hard-hearted. He now stood slightly apart from the rest of the group, to cut their quarry off lest he tried to escape back out of the car park. Marshal observed how the man sniffed and twitched abnormally, either wired on cocaine or itching to start or end the bloody business. Or both. Signet rings decorated heavily scarred knuckles. His expression tightened, like a shrew of a wife about to admonish a

86

tardy husband, as he glared at Marshal. The Irishman's features tightened even more, like a garotte, when Marshal offered up a wry smile in reply.

"You can walk away, driver. He doesn't pay you enough to take a beating for him," Connor Mason said, with a snigger.

"If you wait by the car, Daniel. I shouldn't be too long," Marshal said evenly, fixing his gaze on the boss, whilst also keeping his rottweilers in his peripheral vision. He had the advantage that they would underestimate him. He also owned the advantage of being better than them.

"You're mad," Mason replied, whilst shaking his head, partly amused and partly bemused by the stranger's foolhardy actions.

"I am but mad north-northwest," Marshal replied. Suffice to say, only Ambler recognised the quote from Hamlet.

"You don't have to do this, James. It's my problem," Ambler remarked, whilst retreating towards the Jag. He didn't retreat all the way. Not wanting to completely abandon his friend. There was a scenario where he would give battle too. It was just an unlikely one.

It was not just because Mason didn't pick up on the reference to Hamlet that he decided the time for talk was over. He turned towards Darren and nodded. Giving the order. A piece of gravel scraped beneath his sole on the tarmac as the enforcer advanced.

Marshal altered his stance and raised his hands. A switch had been turned on. Or off. Darren spat and raised his baton. He'd beaten men and women with it alike, like curs, over the past two years since its purchase. He sometimes wondered how it hadn't been bent out of shape.

The soldier would allow his opponent to land the first blow. The baton wasn't a toy, but it wouldn't be a game changer either. Marshal's muscular arm, covered by a shirt and suit jacket, could absorb the blow. He just needed to avoid the steel rod striking his head. Marshal tensed his arm, prepared. The blow smarted, but not that much. Usually, after Darren landed the first blow, his victims cowered or retreated.

He was unprepared for the immediate counterattack. The paratrooper, who had won more than one bout of milling in his regiment, delivered a vicious uppercut. Bone-hard knuckles connected with Darren's fleshy chin. Even from several paces away Ambler heard the thug's teeth click together, as he also bit his tongue, drawing blood. Darren staggered backwards, more than dazed. His eyes were halfway rolled back into his head, about to fall on the ground, when Marshal followed-up with a jab to his nose. Skin splitting. Cartilage crunching. Darren lay on the asphalt. Moving, but barely.

Enraged, Patrick Duggan charged at Marshal, not unlike a bull.

"Bastard," the bouncer said, or snorted. His aim was to bring the driver to the ground. Knock the wind out of him. Straddle him and rain down punches. He hoped that Paddypower would not be far behind in helping to tackle the stranger. They would deal then with the writer - and charge him interest on his debt, so to speak, for their trouble.

If Patrick Duggan resembled a bull, then Marshal acted like a matador as he deftly used his opponent's momentum against him, grabbing the bouncer by the lapels of his jacket, turning his body and throwing him to the ground, as if he were taking part in a judo contest. The asphalt was somewhat firmer than a judo mat, however. The bigger they are the harder they fall. Duggan was immediately winded. Drool ran down his chin. The bull now looked more like a beached whale, as he emitted a death-rattle cum groan - just before Marshal stamped on his throat to remove another piece from the board in the fight.

Liam Quinn liked his nickname. "Paddypower is worth betting on… Paddypower always wins," the ex-boxer would too often joke. In a bare-knuckle brawl, it was the fighter who landed the first punch who would prove the victor, he believed. The Dubliner raised his fists and ejected a gobbet of phlegm from his nose. Marshal raised his fists too, as if about to take part in a boxing match. Quinn, the shorter of the two men, would allow his opponent, aiming to take advantage of his longer reach, to jab first. Quinn believed that he would see the punch coming, through the movement of the driver's eyes and shoulder, and avoid the blow. He would then come inside and deliver a haymaker. The Irishman would follow-up with a flurry of punches, his rings slicing open his opponent's face as if his fists were cheese graters.

Marshal stared the thug straight in the eye, capturing Quinn's aspect like the Ancient Mariner, as he swiftly and surprisingly employed his long leg to kick him in the groin. It wasn't the ex-para's first brawl either. The only rule is that there are no rules. Quinn instinctively grimaced and bent over. As he raised his head again he was struck by an elbow, which broke the skin and cracked his eye socket. "Paddypower" already looked like he wanted to check out, as Marshal put him in a choke hold and rendered him unconscious.

It was now time for Connor Mason to exhibit shock and fear. His men, or two of them, writhed on the ground, like upturned insects. Marshal marched towards the boss. The wronged husband was about to have more wrong done to him. He winced, as if about to cower and cry. He was tempted to offer the driver money to spare him, to beg him not to injure his face. But before any words could splutter out Marshal grabbed him by the hair and dragged him towards the boot of his Jaguar, instructing Mason to get inside the vehicle. Which he did, as if he was a raw recruit and a RSM had given him an order.

With one hand still gripping the Mason's hair, Marshal clicked open the boot. Inside was a torch, toolbox, a muddy pair of wellington boots, spare dog lead and a hidden compartment, from which the driver retrieved a loaded *Sig Sauer p226* pistol.

The temperature dropped once more. But Marshal's voice was colder. It was difficult to tell how much he was playing a sociopath, or how much he was one in earnest. The open boot prevented Ambler, sitting not a little anxiously in the back of the car, from witnessing the scene.

"I used to kill people for a living. Coming out of retirement won't prove a hardship," Marshal remarked, his mouth close to Mason's ear. The barrel of the gun pressed into his temple. "Don't even think about coming after my friend or me again. I know people. I'll tell them about you. I can slot you from the fucking grave if need be. The next time someone holds a gun to your head, they will pull the trigger. Don't lay a hand on your wife, either. I'll find out. Do you understand?" the soldier asked, pressing the gun even more into the trembling man's temple, so it left a circular mark afterwards.

"Yes," Mason said. Whimpering. Urine soaking his tailor-made trousers.

It was difficult to know how much Mason vigorously nodded his head, or how much Marshal moved it. But the wronged husband would take the promise he made to soldier more seriously than any wedding vow.

13.

The carpark resembled the stage at the end of a Greek tragedy as the Jaguar took its leave. Connor Mason's hubris had been checked somewhat. The dogs would soon lick their wounds. Their injuries tempered any zeal to seek redress. None of the fallen had any desire to relive the encounter.

Marshal forgot to indicate as the car turned left, but Ambler understandably forgave the driver for the small, uncharacteristic lapse.

Profuse thanks and apologies initially tumbled out of the usually eloquent author, like an over-exuberant head spilling down a pint glass. But then an air of silence descended like a veil. Ambler bowed his head, in mourning or prayer. Or self-chastisement. He occasionally chewed nails and bit his bottom lip, appearing like a man in need of a cigarette. There was a period when he glared dumbly out of the window, as if wanting to remember or forget something of immense importance. Ambler frequently glanced at his phone, expecting or desiring a message to take his mind off things. Sometimes his hand trembled as he clasped the device.

They drove through a less salubrious part of London. Lights flickered in takeaway windows. Some on purpose, some not. Foxes had ripped rubbish sacks apart. A few shops were boarded up. Others you might wish could close. Couples held hands. Fat people held grease-smeared boxes of chicken and chips. Delivery drivers raced through red lights. Most folk glared at their phones, even if in company.

Marshal kept an eye on his friend in the mirror. He had witnessed thousand-yard stares and bystanders in shock before. A hundred thoughts were probably attempting to pass through the junction of his mind, but there was only room for a half a dozen or so. He appeared haunted like a condemned man, when really he was a recipient of a last minute pardon. The driver switched on some music in an attempt to restore a degree of normalcy.

"I'm just an old chunk of coal
But I'm going to be a diamond some day."

The music barely registered. As hungry as Ambler felt he knew he wouldn't be able to keep down any food. He was too distracted to notice how his back was aching as well. He continually turned over in his mind, like a baker kneading dough, whether he should tell his new employers about what had just transpired. Answers would lead to more questioning. The operation could get called off. His chance to do some potential good in the world would fade, quicker than a politician's promise. What they didn't know couldn't hurt them, though, Ambler reasoned. Spying is deception.

They eventually got to Kensington. But it didn't feel like home.

Marshal had already sent a message to his dogsitter to ask if she could look after Violet overnight. It would cost him a few quid, but it would be worth it. Marshal didn't offer and Ambler didn't ask, but the driver would get drunk with his friend and sleep on the sofa again.

The author switched on an antique lamp, which he had bought with his ex-wife when they were newlyweds. The two men sat in the living-room. Marshal did his best to look at ease, to put his friend at ease too.

"Whisky?" Ambler asked.

"Aye," Marshal replied.

"Graham Greene called it the "medicine of despair". I'm too tired to disagree with him," the author said, as he poured two large measures. Ambler thought, however, how Kierkegaard and Sara would argue that faith was the medicine of despair.

A short silence ensued, pregnant with all manner of unvoiced thoughts, before the quiet became too deafening for Ambler and he had to speak again:

"Quite a night, no?"

The author, soon to be turned spy, noticed how dusty his bookshelves were as he spoke. He really needed a cleaner and some fresh air.

"I've had duller ones," the ex-para drily replied, craving humour after violence like some crave a cigarette after sex.

"I don't know how to thank you, repay you," Ambler emitted, his voice breaking from emotion or a dry throat. A swig or two of the *Talisker* cured the latter, though. His hand no longer trembled but Ambler winced, recalling the terror he felt when Mason stood before him, believing he was Russian. It was worse than any nightmare he had suffered - and would haunt him for longer. He would wince as well, remembering the sound of his friend breaking bones. A man gargling, from having his throat stamped on.

"It's all part of the service. No need to even tip me."

Ambler didn't quite know whether to admire or worry about his friend in relation to his nonchalant attitude towards what had happened. A tiny spot of blood marked Marshal's cheek, but Ambler felt too awkward about mentioning it.

"I barely knew who she was, let alone who her husband was," the adulterer protested, although Veronica had dropped a few telling hints if Ambler chose to listen. Not that Marshal judged him in any way. The soldier himself had conducted affairs with more than one married woman over the years. Probably more than he even knew. Few people spoke about the equality of the sexes in regard to a woman's capacity to deceive - and lust. "Do you think that he will now come after me, us?"

"Not if he knows what's good for him. He may think he's a hawk, but he's a dove. Yet if you suspect something just drop me a line."

Marshal didn't want to admit it to his friend, or himself, but it had felt good tonight. Painters must paint, writers must write, soldiers must fight.

Ambler nodded his head, in acknowledgement and gratitude. He also thought how, if Mason should cross his path again, he would talk to his new employers. He was a valued asset, at least until the operation was over. MI6 had attack dogs who could put the fear of living God into the man even more than Marshal, if that was at all possible.

Another pause. Another swig. Another sigh.

"My life flashed before my eyes in that car park, I can tell you," Ambler confessed. "I was thoroughly unimpressed and underwhelmed," he added, half-jokingly.

Marshal was pleased to notice that glibness/normalcy were returning.

Ambler did his best not to stay up too late or drink too much. His best was, just about, good enough. He told Marshal that he would not need him the following day, explaining that he had a meeting to attend but it was in walking distance. Ambler didn't feel particularly good about lying to the man who had just risked his life for him. But he reasoned that it would have been worse if he didn't feel guilty.

Before drifting off to sleep Ambler received a message from Samantha, informing him that she would be free to "do brunch" the following day. Her hotel was a fifteen-minute walk away. They would have brunch, or leave half of it, to then go up to her room. She accompanied the message with a couple of photographs, dressed in two different cocktail dresses. She wanted Ambler's advice of which outfit she should wear for an upcoming party. She looked good. Better than good. Great. Displaying just the right amount of bronzed fleshed in all the right places. She was half expecting, half demanding Ambler to attend to her. Potemkin to her Catherine the Great. He should scamper over to her and be brought to heel. It had happened before. If he refused her then she might look to be courted by another suitor.

"I do not believe in second chances," she had once asserted, in between drags on a cigarette, Ambler recalled. Even when her features were as hard as obsidian, she was uncommonly beautiful. As addictive as any drug that's bad for you.

But Ambler was beginning to believe in second chances. He just hoped that God and Maria did too. He would keep his word and meet with Birch the following day, rather than see Samantha. It was a novel feeling for the writer, for duty to eclipse desire.

14.

The neighbourhood reeked of wealth and vulgarity. He couldn't keep track of the number of overpriced restaurants, estate agents and shops selling handbags that cost more than the price of a decent second-hand car. Ambler glanced around, with differing degrees of subtlety, to check if anyone was following him. Whether they were doing so on the orders of Connor Mason or Viktor Rybin. Or Simon Birch. Most of the lissom, surgically enhanced women were honeytraps, regardless of if they worked for an intelligence agency or not, the author wryly thought. His back was a tad stiff, but Ambler had more important things on his mind. Any pain was de-prioritised, like moving a literary novel down one's "to be read" pile.

I'm a joe. But hopefully no ordinary joe, Ambler joked, as he walked towards the Knightsbridge address, akin to a man who was either attending a job interview or a sentence hearing. The writer recalled interviewing an ex-spook once, for research for a novel, who spoke about his handling of operatives.

"We are asked to trust those who we must instinctively distrust... Joes can be perverts, prima-donnas, fantasists, cowards. Or human beings, as we call them. Our joes have probably had a few choice names for their handlers over the years too, ranging from angels to demons. We can start off blackmailing a joe to the refrain of all manner of protests and curses, but then end up delivering him to a chorus of thanks... One can tap into a joe's ego or fear, but for the most part money talks when recruiting an asset. Not everyone is a Gordievsky. One usually needs to pay someone to do the right thing in this world. There is currency in trust and loyalty, but all too often currency is currency... If there is a typical joe he is probably divorced - or would like to be divorced. He is probably embittered, for being passed over for a promotion. Or life has treated him unfairly. He is spending beyond his means, perhaps because he is keeping a mistress as well as a wife and family. He drives a car he hates, or one he can ill afford. He is disillusioned, having realised that communism or another addled ideology may not be the promised land. He is asking questions of himself and his country. A handler should be there at the right time to provide the right answers to those questions... Recruiting is an art rather than science. One should give a joe a narrative he can believe in - or one should pretend to believe in the story he has gifted himself. A handler's neck muscles should initially ache when meeting a potential recruit, from nodding in agreement. Convince him that he is the hero in his own story. Feed their ego and fill their coffers. One should imply that there is an entire team dedicated to his welfare, twenty-five hours a day, eight days a week. The handler is but the tip of the spear... Tell them that all will be well, even when it may not be. Or especially when it may not be. Some joes crave attention, drama. But they should act normally. It's the distressed fish that the shark will always go for... A joe will only prove so valuable for so long. He will only have so many miles on the clock, before he breaks down or one has to pension him off... Despite the dynamic and dichotomy between a joe and his handler, however, there are plenty of similarities. We do not just share the traits that we often have a drinking problem or failed marriage. Handlers can be guilty of thinking that they can change the world too. Handlers can be guilty of serving Mammon rather than God, because they have a mistress and wife to keep in clover. It's difficult to fund a private sector lifestyle on public sector pay... Handlers can become delusional. Handlers can be turned, like a boat with a faulty rudder. Just look at that bastard, Philby... The cardinal rule is to trust no one in life as well as espionage."

Ambler pictured the former spy, one Alexander Drake, as he visited him in his townhouse in Salisbury. Drake claimed to be a friend and neighbour to the late Ted Heath, which didn't particularly endear him to the author or anyone else. Blood vessels had burst upon his cheeks and nose, appearing like maps of the Mississippi delta. Pronounced, patrician features projected an air of imperiousness. Yet his rheumy eyes and languid movements bespoke of a sense of boredom. His outfit had been cleaned and ironed (by a housekeeper that reminded Drake of his nanny). The retired spy, who had written a self-published history of the Edwardian Age, looked like a cross between an elderly Benedick Cumberbatch and Jacob Rees-Mogg. His voice was as patrician as his features. He wore a linen suit, replete with a paisley pocket square, and brown, polished brogues - which he often inspected and removed any speck of dust from. A mane of pomaded grey hair sat on top of a domed forehead. He cut an elegant but lonely, pouting figure. Queer, in more than one sense of the word. Ambler noted how he was often critical of his female colleagues in the service. Those who were superior in rank to the intelligence officer often lacked judgement - especially when they disagreed with him. Americans were "ghastly" - the French "ghastlier - a bitter tasting cocktail of ignorance and arrogance". The Russians were "ruthless, cunning and wrong-headed". The Chinese "are crass, peddling tat and a message and culture that will never take root in the West... They are the new Victorians and colonialists, but lack Dickens, cricket and class... They have no respect or perhaps even concept of the individual - and everyone wants to be an individual nowadays, unfortunately." Foreign Secretaries "should stick to just writing cheques rather than memos." Prime Ministers "should just do what they're told and not ask too many questions, lest they hear answers that they would prefer not to." For all of Alexander Drake's nasally talk of doom and declinism, however, Ambler thought that the spy cut a comical figure. He was, like a politician, his own satire. Or beyond satire. *Life is still a joke. Or maybe a cruel joke,* the novelist mused as he travelled back to London from Salisbury.

The unassuming two-storey house was located in an anonymous looking mews, five minutes' walk from *Harrod's*. The curtains were drawn, as if hermetically sealing the property. Four empty milk bottles sat outside of the black door, which the normally non-clumsy Ambler nearly knocked over. Were they part of a crude security measure? Did the number of bottles act as a code to signify the status of the safehouse? Who orders in their milk nowadays? People like Alexander Drake, Ambler conceded.

He pressed the bell. Although he sensed there was someone behind the door, it was a minute until it opened. Pins and needles sprang up in his feet. His back throbbed like a lovestruck heart. Thoughts prickled, again. He was anxious once more about whether his new employers were aware of what had transpired last night. He did not want to get caught up in a truth or a lie. He strongly suspected that his handlers remained in the dark, but he did not know for sure. Ambler the writer was keen on irony, ambiguity, red herrings and sudden reveals. Ambler the joe, however, craved certainty. He was greeted by Birch. A brief smile was succeeded by a more formal, business-like expression. His expression betrayed either everything or nothing.

The house was spacious, comfortable and forgettable. The author's gimlet eye surveyed the interior but there was nothing to take in of note. Birch led him into a windowless dining cum meeting room at the rear of the property, where two other middle-aged white men were waiting for them. Polite smiles and firm handshakes accompanied the introductions. Civility tamped down any divots of anxiety or wariness.

Ambler was initially introduced to Edward Palmer. Government lawyer. Clean-shaven. Jermyn St shirt. Narrow head. His designer glasses looked expensive and were expensive. He had a slight tan and courteous, obliging manner. Palmer was only unfair and unpleasant when being litigious. He told himself that he was only doing his job, when complicit in the task to ruin a person's life. Otherwise, Palmer was a consummate gentleman. Part of his job was to put joes at ease. Exude trust and competence. Married to Phoebe, who he at met at university. Two children. Timothy and Emily. A dog - Xerxes. Cottage in Cornwall, which they could afford not to rent out. Palmer had spent the morning, after going over the file on Daniel Ambler that Birch had given him, drafting an email to one of Timothy's teachers at the prep school, asking him to re-consider the mark they issued to his son for a recent exam. Palmer had attended a charity auction the evening before. His wife helped campaign for the Tunbridge Wells chapter of an organisation dedicated to re-joining the EU. Their slogan, which was far from catchy or clear, was "Re-Join, not Purloin." Edward often rolled his eyes behind his wife's back when she spoke about what the charity was doing on their Facebook message board, but he showed his support last night by bidding for a spa weekend in Rye.

"We will shortly ask you to sign a specially amended Official Secrets Act. It's there for your protection as well as ours. Edward can answer any questions about the document and furnish you with impartial advice. We are still governed by procedure and compliance, just like any branch of the civil service. The law still applies to us," Birch remarked, without a hint of irony when spouting the phrase "impartial advice". Ambler also remembered, on several occasions, when the MI6 operative had boasted how the law didn't apply to elements of his service.

"Don't worry, Mr Ambler, you will not be signing your life away. I can answer any questions you might have," Palmer remarked, like a non-partisan BBC journalist. Politely. Reassuringly. Like Birch, the lawyer spoke with an upper middle-class or lower upper-class accent. It would have come as little surprise to the novelist if a forked tongue tasted the air, after he spoke. During his divorce, after dealing with his own solicitor and Sara's, Ambler had purchased a special portrait of Shakespeare, with the accompanying quote underneath:

"The first thing we do, let's kill all the lawyers."

Ambler noted the document and stainless-steel fountain pen on the glass table in front of him. He fleetingly thought himself akin to Faust. About to sign away his soul. He just didn't know whether Birch, Palmer or some unseen figure was Mephistopheles. Was Sara his Margarete? Yet Ambler also thought about how he was here to win back his soul. Or Sara. Perhaps they were one in the same thing.

The second man was Frank Tanner. Tanner wore a suit, but it didn't fit as snugly as the others in the room. Military bearing. Barrel chest. Shrewd, or suspicious, eyes. Shortish hair (though the former soldier considered it long, for him). Greying stubble. Yellow teeth, from too much coffee rather than nicotine over the years. Stolid. Ex-SAS. Former Special Branch. Cottage in Hereford. Married twice. First time to a hairdresser, second to a stewardess. Patriot. The army had been the only real home and family he'd felt comfortable and content in. He knew what it was like to be shot - and to shoot someone. Willing to die for his brothers-in-arms on the battlefield, but not easy to live with at home. Ambler noted the man's remarkably strong, square jaw. It was either the jaw of a man one could trust, or a fascist. Polished shoes. Tanner maybe even polished his belt buckle, as if he were still in the army. His handshake was close to being vice-like. Tanner was not altogether pleased on being called in at short notice, cutting off a fly-fishing trip, to train up the "civilian" - a term he often used, with a sneer.

"Tanner is the best in the business, in relation to training our personnel. Not that we foresee any problems arising. It's just better to be safe than sorry. You may even just call it a box-ticking exercise," Simon Birch argued. Again, a brief smile was followed a more business-like expression.

"Just keep in mind what I teach you and you will be fine, Mr Ambler. This is not some game or adventure. Patience and professionalism will see us through. There will be no kiss kiss bang bang. You are stepping up to do your duty. I respect that. I will take you through some basic tradecraft, not that I am envisioning that you'll need to utilise any of the lessons I teach you. But as Mr Birch said, it's better to be safe than sorry," Tanner said, in a mixed accent that betrayed how much he had moved around as a foster child and then soldier, before taking several gulps of coffee from a Leeds Utd mug that no one else dared drink from in the house. "We are pressed for time, but Mr Birch assures me you will be a quick study."

Ambler was tempted to say that it was like being back for the first day of school, but that there was no danger of anyone stealing his lunch money. He rightly judged that the joke would fall flat -

and feared receiving a glare from Tanner that looked like he might steal his lunch money, or worse.

"But first things first. Edward, you have the floor," Birch remarked, moving aside for the lawyer to glide past and place a manicured finger on an A4 spiral bound book. A contract. The Official Secrets Act. Or a specially drafted version for their joe.

"The service runs on paperwork, Daniel, just like any other. Before we can continue, I must ask you to read and sign this document. You have doubtless signed one or two non-disclosure agreements during your time as an author. Just think of this as a glorified NDA. I can answer any questions you might have. Feel free to take your time to read over. We ask all our associates to sign a version of the Official Secrets Act. It's standard practice, as you can imagine," Palmer said, giving the impression that he had Ambler's interests at heart, as much as he did his employer. Technically he was not lying when he stated that MI6 made all its associates sign a version of the Official Secrets Act, but the document in front of their newest asset contained plenty of non-standard clauses, ones which the lawyer would have re-drafted or removed before even considering putting a signature to the document himself. The novelist would not be signing his life away, but he would be abdicating certain rights and freedoms. But Palmer was just doing his job. The government, rather than the poor soul in front of him, paid his salary. The lawyer sometimes thought how Britain had signed certain rights and freedoms away during its membership of the European Union, but the civil servant would dare not openly admit such a thought, or heresy, to his wife or work colleagues.

Birch reiterated to his friend, or his joe, that he should take his time when "perusing" the document. That did not discourage the handler from standing over him impatiently, waiting for Ambler to sign. Putting pen to paper would move the operation forward. It would also put his old college rival under his authority. Control.

The black ink was fresh on the paper, Ambler thought. There were sections in red which glistened like blood. The writer was familiar with most of the legalise in the document. "No liability...

tortious... prosecution." He had signed plenty of book contracts in the past, which had granted a portion of his life to his publishers (although none of them had contained the phrase "treasonous"). MI6 would now own another slice of his existence. But it was for the greater good.

Palmer and Tanner also loomed over Ambler as he sat and read the "paperwork", pen in hand. He could smell the coffee on the ex-soldier's breath and the lawyer's florid cologne.

At least, it appeared, they had no knowledge of the events of yesternight, Ambler thought. It felt like a small victory. Perhaps God would favour his endeavour, he mused - as he signed and initialled the document in various places.

But God can be as capricious as good luck, or most women.

"Right, let's get to work," Tanner announced, clapping and rubbing his hands before the ink had even dried.

15.

Far from being handed a *Walther PPK* or the keys to an *Aston Martin DB5*, Ambler was presented with a couple of manilla folders containing background information and intelligence on Viktor Rybin. He was asked to just sit and work his way through the files for an hour. Reading. It felt like a busman's holiday. Spying is collating. Some of the intelligence in the files Ambler was already aware of, some he suspected. No one made any serious money in Russia with greasing someone's palm and/or getting blood on their hands. Several paragraphs in the files had been redacted. Large strips of black ink served as an electric fence and a sign. Keep Out.

"I am afraid that some information is need to know," Birch explained, not with a little satisfaction - in putting his old friend in his place. The successful novelist and womaniser lived in his world now.

Ambler was going to counter that, surely, if anyone needed to know it was himself. But he merely pursed his lips, turned his head and rolled his eyes. Ambler was not immune to experiencing shards of contempt for Birch in a personal capacity. The new asset sensed that he would also experience similar feelings towards his handler in a professional capacity before they got to the end of the operation.

Despite hankering after something stronger, Ambler was offered tea, coffee or bottled water. His eyes soon ached more than his back. The prose sparkled about as much as a black hole. He read on, however, like he was back in college, revising for an exam.

Ambler rubbed his eyes from tiredness, rather than disbelief, after going through the files. Palmer asked him a few questions related to the intelligence, to ensure the new recruit had taken in the contents of the files.

Birch proceeded to then brief Ambler on the operation. They were no longer friends. They were handler and joe.

"We will run through things in greater detail after we receive the all-clear to go live with the operation. But you will fly to Havana. Your cover will be a research trip for a novel which you are about to write. You will travel to Vetrov's villa. He will arrange for a car to pick you up. When you meet with Vetrov you will let him set the agenda. If he wants to play the magnanimous host, let him. On the surface of things, you are just two old friends meeting once more. Your meeting may last a couple of hours. Or it may be the case that he wants you to stay overnight. Get drunk together if need be. Be grateful for his sacrifice. Britain thanks him. Russia will thank him. Flatter him… Reassure him that we will honour all his wishes and he is in control… The most important thing is to leave the villa with the file, which will be contained on a flash drive. Your safety is also of paramount concern for us, of course," Birch remarked, the last sentence coming as an afterthought. "It goes without saying, though I will say it anyway, that under no circumstances should you attempt to access the file yourself. When you travel back into the city you will check into the *Inglaterra Hotel*. You will be met outside the hotel by one of our operatives. It may sound like a scene from one of your novels, but he will ask you for a light. You will hand the flash drive over to him… You will spend the next couple of days substantiating your cover, after which you will fly home… We have assets and support we can call upon in Cuba, but by activating and alerting them we may cause that which we wish to prevent… Your presence should produce as little fuss and attention as possible… I am pleased to report, also, that there has been an absence of chatter in relation to Vetrov being a person of interest for the regime," Birch said, reassuringly. Although a colleague suggested that this could be an alarming sign. If Vetrov was a person of interest, they would not wish to show their hand. Birch dismissed the theory, believing that his rival was just jealous that he was not taking a lead on the operation. "When you return, Daniel, do not contact us. We will contact you. But you will be greeted with a hero's welcome, eventually, I'm sure… Any immediate questions?"

Ambler doubtless had more questions that Birch would provide answers for, but his most pressing enquiry related to when he would be called to depart. When would he need to get his affairs in order, so to speak?

"Soon," Birch replied.

"Could you be any vaguer?" Ambler countered, partly in good humour. It was perhaps too much to ask for the novelist not to be sarcastic or glib throughout the entire afternoon.

Whether he was looking at his old friend or new joe his mask slipped, and Simon Theodore Birch did not appear best pleased. It was like they were back in *The White Hart* in Oxford again and Ambler had just made a joke at Birch's expense in front of a pretty barmaid. There was a brief but notable awkward silence. Tanner could hear the ticking of his *Breitling* watch.

Egos. It's all about egos, Palmer thought - although he would often explain to colleagues that it was all about "due process". The lawyer had lost count of the number of times he had been present in the room, with higher-ups in the intelligence services and government, discussing matters of national security. The clash of civilisations descended into fractious clashes of personalities. Department heads would attempt to guard their patch or feather their nests. Petty slights (real or imagined) and disagreements from years gone by would re-emerge and fuel major decision making, or more often than not prevent any decision making. They thought themselves big beasts in the jungle, but really they were mere preening peacocks. Palmer also thought about how he hoped his wife would be out for the evening so he could watch what he wanted to on the television.

"We will inform Vetrov's emissary that you are willing to meet. You will hopefully sympathise that our budgets do not stretch to purchasing a crystal ball. We will be at the mercy of Vetrov and his emissary replying in their own time. So, as mentioned, the answer is still soon," Birch remarked, curtly - or cattily.

"I think that'll be enough for one day," Tanner posited. The intelligence officer didn't need to use his considerable training to recognise that there was a splinter of tension in the air. "You have already had a lot to take in. We will have a full day tomorrow too."

No rest for the weary, Ambler mused - thinking how he might use the phrase he had just come up with in his next novel.

"Well done today, Daniel. I understand all that you must be going through. Just follow the instructions we give you and all will be fine," Birch said, not a little patronisingly, as he showed Ambler to the door. Ambler fancied how his friend had probably been waiting twenty years to talk to him in such a condescending manner. He hoped that it had been worth the wait.

The joe took a deep breath and let the cool air wash against his cheeks. Or, rather than a joe, could he not be considered a full-fledged spook? Or, given his brief with Vetrov, was he not going to be a handler? He sighed, not quite knowing whether he wanted to have a drink or sleep. He pulled out his phone. The device had seemingly been vibrating, on silent, the entire day - as if it needed a sedative. There was a whole raft of text messages and emails. His inbox was full of over a dozen manuscripts and cover letters, forwarded on by Gordon Turner or sent direct, from members of the group. The would-be writers, some trusting their dreams to him, didn't matter much to him last night. They mattered, along with a whole raft of things, even less to Ambler at present. He received messages from his publisher and agent, as well as invites to launch parties, dinners and a literary festival. He received a text message and voicemail from Veronica, but staunchly ignored them. *Delete them.* The editor of *The Tablet* asked him to write an article on the demise of the "Catholic literary novel", whatever that was. His accountant asked him to chase and send some VAT receipts. Samantha sent a photo of the view from her hotel room, albeit most of the image was taken up of her in an elegant cocktail dress. The only message he replied to was one from Marshal, who asked if Ambler could pay him cash in hand. The grateful client felt he owed the driver more than he could ever repay - and wrote back that he would arrange to meet in a day or two, depending on his schedule. Ambler's thumb also hung over the buttons of his Blackberry as he tried to concoct an excuse to see Sara. He was a novelist in need of a plot device. His brain felt too fuzzy, though, and he put the phone back in his pocket. Most of the messages were tantamount to spam. The real world was but a walking shadow. It was the shadowlands of espionage - the mission - which mattered now.

But perhaps the world of shadows was becoming *too* real for Ambler. The cadence of his breathing and heart altered. He was on edge - Alice through the looking glass. His temples and palms began to secrete sweat. He watched for any curtain twitchers and stared down the mews for any parked Range Rovers. Or black taxis. A spook once told him how the FSB had purchased a fleet of black cabs, to move expediently and anonymously around London. No one gave them a second look, aside from Ambler now. Were there any with their lights off but failing to carry any passengers? The new joe was Schrodinger's Cat, acting as if he was and wasn't being followed at the same time. It was incredibly unlikely that his cover had been blown, but how could he know for certain? He wasn't entirely jittery, but still Ambler would flittingly glance in parked car wing mirrors and reflective shop windows for anyone trailing him. God help him if a car backfired to sound like a gunshot. The nervous joe might empty his bowels, faster than a Russian gangster could order a bottle of *Cristal*. Birch and Tanner had repeatedly reassured their new asset that he should not worry. They would know if there were any Russian wet squads in the capital. But how? Even, given the worst-case scenario, if Ambler became a target, they blithely asserted that they could protect him. But how? Like they protected Berezovsky? Or Sergei and Yulia Skripal? Ambler could read between the lines, the ones redacted or otherwise. If Viktor Rybin wanted you eliminated, then sooner or later you would be. Ironically, the Russian was like a US Marshal. He always got his man. MI6's own intelligence reports revealed that Rybin had given the order to assassinate the enemies of Russia on British soil before. The former (or current) FSB agent would not lose sleep, Ambler imagined, over doing so again.

"Nothing can or will go wrong. We have a plan in place," Birch insisted at one point, swotting away, like a one-winged-gnat, any concerns Ambler might have harboured.

But Man plans, God laughs. Whether it was a Jewish or Catholic God. As tight a ship as Birch might claim to be a part of, the operation could be as leaky as a sieve. All it needed was for a one disaffected, or greedy, member of the Russian oligarch's personnel to make a phone call to Moscow and disclose Vetrov's intentions. The entire operation could be a Trojan horse too. Karla-like. Ambler could be being used as a courier to feed false information to MI6. The service would trumpet their intelligence coup to the Americans. But the treasure would ultimately be proved worthless, fool's gold, and trust between the western allies would erode. The special relationship would be less special. Members of the Five Eyes alliance would observe one another with caution and suspicion, much to Russia's satisfaction.

Ambler slowly, or carefully, walked from Knightsbridge back to Kensington. The journey felt like it was uphill. When he reached his flat, he found that he couldn't sleep. But he could drink. Drink would wash away the thoughts of real or imaginary wet squads. Drink would take the edge off. He remembered how he had a bottle of twenty-four-year-old *Macallan* single malt squirreled away for a special occasion. When he purchased the bottle, Ambler promised that he would open it at the birth of his first son or daughter. Or when one of his books made it into *The New York Times* bestseller lists. But now felt like as good a time as any. *It would be a small tragedy if I died before opening it*, he wryly posed.

DUTY CALLS

16.

Ambler slept fitfully, as one might expect. Curiosity got the better of him and he found himself checking out the location of Vetrov's villa online in the middle of the night. Although owned by a former Russian oligarch, the property was not as expansive and lavish as one might have imagined. Although situated just beyond the outskirts of Havana, it appeared relatively remote. The grounds were walled and gated. The main house was a two-storey building and must have contained around five bedrooms. A swimming pool, next to a small guesthouse, could be seen between the leafy trees which populated the images of the estate. Ambler wondered if the house was kitted with CCTV. The cream-coloured walls looked like they were scalable.

The spy novelist retrieved his copy of *Our Man in Havana*, which was sitting on a shelf in his bedroom. It was a near perfect novel, if such a description existed, with seldom a wasted paragraph or line. As good as *The End of the Affair*, *The Human Factor* and *The Quiet American*. Greene was one of the few novelists who Ambler regularly re-read. *Our Man in Havana* captured the absurdism and folly inherent in espionage, as well its darker shades. Spies can be foolish, conceited characters. Just like anyone else. Ambler thumbed through the pages of the paperback and noted a quote he had underlined:

"You should dream more, Mr Wormold. Reality in our century is not something to be faced."

He also recalled the pitch perfect movie adaptation. Shot in black and white, the film still captured the colours of the city. If there was a greater actor than Alec Guinness, then Ambler struggled to think of one. Guinness knew how to be both an individual and anonymous. The Catholic actor, who played Smiley with assiduity, might have made an accomplished spy himself, Ambler idly fancied.

He drifted back to sleep for an hour - and was woken by the abrasive squawk of his alarm. Ambler couldn't remember the last time he had to be up so early, for something genuinely important. He even made himself some breakfast. Another rare occurrence. Ambler mustered himself to attack the day - before the day attacked him.

The morning air was bracing as he made his way from Kensington to Knightsbridge once more. He was perfunctory, at best, when replying to a few messages on his phone. He was due to save the world, he joked to himself. It didn't matter if the actor to read his next audiobook had an Irish lilt or not.

Ambler winced, cringed and cursed himself as he clumsily kicked a milk bottle over outside the door of the safehouse. Thankfully it didn't smash, though the sound drew more than one curtain twitcher. Should Palmer have stepped out the door, appearing unaccustomedly disgruntled, Ambler would have asked if the document he signed yesterday covered medical insurance for dyspraxia.

Tanner answered, appearing characteristically disgruntled. If anything, his poker face twitched with a mite more resentment than usual for the good-humoured spy novelist. He sighed-cum-snorted and then ground his teeth, causing his square jaw to become squarer. The collars on the operative's shirt were religiously starched, as stiff as stocks worn by Redcoats Ambler fancied. Again, his shoes and belt buckle seemed freshly polished.

Frank Tanner was something of a legend in the service, unbeknownst to the new joe. He was considered one of the best watchers and streetwalkers of his generation. He had an unblemished record of never losing sight of a target - or revealing to a subject that he was under observation. He made any personnel raise their game, who he worked with. He drilled his teams hard - and then would drink hard with them and celebrate once the operation was over. Stories abounded about Tanner, which he seldom bothered to ever confirm or deny. Tanner was off duty one day when he noticed a Pakistani youth come out of a mosque in North London, carrying a backpack, displaying an array of indicators relating to a terrorist threat. He followed the adolescent to a house in Neasden, where he called a contact to ask if the house or any of its inhabitants were on a suspected terrorist list. They were. Tanner joined the team of armed officers who secured the property and apprehended the five jihadists inside, who were a day away from placing half a dozen nail bombs in various major train stations throughout the capital. Tanner took it as his personal responsibility to locate and restrain the youth he tracked from the mosque, "accidentally" dislocating the teenager's shoulder and breaking his jaw as he did so.

"Do you think that you used appropriate force?" one colleague, fresh from completing a PHD at a less than respected university, asked a week later.

"No. I should have slotted the bastard and lessened the jihadist population of the country by one. But, unfortunately, I used inappropriate force."

"Do you know that what you did could be construed as "racially profiling" the suspect?"

"Yes, thank you. It's why we got the win," the former soldier replied, with a smile as broad as his chest, deliberately re-interpreting the pointed criticism as a compliment.

Tanner led Ambler into the meeting room, where a tired and slightly irritable looking Birch was waiting. His tie didn't quite match his suit and shirt and a penny-sized coffee-stain marked his trousers. Birch had waited up the previous evening for Hamilton to return home from dinner at the *Carlton Club*, so he could give his superior a quick debrief.

"How was he?" Hamilton asked, pleased that they had secured the author's signature. With the contract Palmer had drafted, they now owned their courier. "He's indentured."

"We'll knock him into shape," Birch replied, implying that his friend was somehow deficient. The handler could therefore take greater credit if, or rather when, the operation succeeded.

Not only did Birch retire to bed after midnight, next to his snoring wife, but he had to rouse himself early in the morning. He resented how it was only a short walk from Kensington for his joe. Birch failed to greet Ambler like an old school friend. He didn't even offer to pour his new colleague a coffee from the steaming pot on the table, after pouring one for himself.

"Right, we're here. Let's start," Tanner said. Time was a commodity that he didn't like to squander. "I will be running through some basic training today. Mr Birch will brief you on some other aspects of the operation. I should state that what I will teach you is procedural and precautionary. There is no need to worry. If all goes as expected, I do not believe that you will be called upon to utilise any of your training."

There was almost a mathematical algorithm in use. The more that Tanner and Birch told their joe that he shouldn't worry, the more he started to. *Trust no one,* had been the mantra of more than one intelligence officer the author had encountered over the years. Ambler received the distinct impression that something was being kept from him. There were moments when he believed that Tanner and Birch were offering each other conspiratorial looks, especially when he asked about the Russian presence in Havana, but the novelist may have just had an overactive imagination. It was not what a spook told you, but what he didn't tell you, which mattered. Spying is second-guessing.

Tanner proceeded to project a series of maps onto the white wall facing Ambler. Holding an old-fashioned drillmaster's stick, rather than a laser pointer, Tanner marked out some key locations for the joe: the airport, the address of his hotel, Vetrov's villa. Tanner also flagged up where the British Embassy was in Havana, as well as a safe house manned by a trusted operative.

"Memorise these addresses. And then remember them again, every day. If something goes awry, which it won't, these are your ports in the storm… We will alert certain personnel that we are running an asset, although they will only be aware of the callsign of the operation and your codename. They will not ask about your mission - and you should not divulge it, without first receiving authorisation from Mr Birch. Do you understand?"

Ambler nodded.

"We have designated the mission *Operation Pancho Villa.* The name should divert any suspicion away from the Russianist nature of the business at hand," Birch remarked, pleased with his small contribution. "Your codename will be Potter."

Wizard, Ambler drily replied in his head rather than out loud. The novelist in him would have preferred the name "Wormold", the hero of Greene's *Our Man in Havana*.

"We will also get you to memorise a phone number, which you can call should you fall into any difficulties. Which you won't, of course," Tanner stated, before taking another large gulp of coffee.

Birch was right about one thing. Ambler was a quick study - and not just because he was familiar with some operational details from researching his novels over the years. The world of espionage wasn't completely alien or frightening to the new joe. No, not completely.

Tanner would often ask if Ambler understood his instructions - and would test him at random to recount addresses and elements of *Operation Pancho Villa* they had discussed earlier in the day - but the joe was equal to the task. The gruff intelligence officer would scrunch up his already narrow eyes in scrutiny and suspicion at the novelist, before moving on. Satisfied. Or satisfied enough. The courier was also shown photographs of "friendlies" - assets in Havana at the British Embassy and safe house. Some of the wan, white visages looked like they would have fitted in well at *The Blackheath Writing Society*. One looked like a pervert, who cared little if he got caught as his aristocratic father could afford a lawyer for his second son. Another, a crapulent war correspondent whose best days were behind him. Ex-wives outnumbered his scoops.

Purely just "out of precaution" Tanner presented his joe with a crimson folder containing images of suspected kill squad operatives, associated with assassinations connected to Viktor Rybin. Ambler's stomach churned as he turned through the photographs and snippets of intelligence. He understandably took even greater care memorising the Russian personnel, who might damn him, as opposed to the British faces, who might deliver him.

It was a rogue's gallery, of course. The photos resembled mugshots. They made Connor Mason's thugs look like lipstick lesbians. There were more cauliflower ears than on a boxing undercard, more shaven heads than at a meeting of the Bruce Willis Appreciation Society. Expressions were cruel, or pitiless. Their mothers had trouble loving them, no doubt. Many already looked like they wanted to murder Ambler, as they stared out at him from the folder. A few torso shots displayed muscular bodies dripping with elaborate tattoos, often containing religious iconography. Gold teeth were prevalent. Even from just the grainy images he could smell the kvass and vodka on their breath. Many were ex-army or FSB. There was one Andrey Morozov, who looked like and was an unashamed rapist - and not the Premier League footballer or disc jockey kind. Morozov, who had more than one alias, was wanted in Prague for the sexual assault and murder of a young prostitute. The file reported that the operative, a known associate of Viktor Rybin, was responsible for half a dozen assassinations in Georgia and Chechnya in the past five years. Tattoos of Byzantine crosses adorned scarred knuckles. He resembled a sinister-looking Bernard Bresslaw, Ambler fancied. In contrast, there was Roman Zaitsev - who looked like Anthony Valentine, when he starred in the TV series *Raffles*. The file recounted how Zaitsev had acted as a honeytrap on at least two occasions, seducing male and female MEPs. He was handsome, cultured and a specialist in using nerve agents. The main photograph in the file had the blond Russian holding up a champagne glass in a toast, around a dinner at a London restaurant, surrounded by a bevy of satin-wearing women and a prominent Tory minister. The intelligence report stated how Zaitsev often worked as a conduit between Rybin and various top-flight lawyers and financial PR agencies in the capital. Ambler wondered what he might do, if he glimpsed the likes of Morozov or Zaitsev through a crowd in Havana. Perhaps it would be preferable just to die of fear, before being abducted, tortured and shot.

"Now, you may be wondering what you should do if you somehow catch sight of any un-friendlies," Tanner remarked, sounding as if he had drunk a pint of gravel the night before. "The answer is, do not engage. Retreat rather than surrender. Run if you have to. Find a safe, public space if you are unable to reach the secure locations I have given you. Don't get any ideas about being a hero. Be a coward, so you can tell yourself that you're a hero at a later date. You're not a character in one of your novels. Keep your phone on you at all times. It'll serve a tracking device, or homing beacon. Not that we have any fears about having to use it as one. All will be well."

It was at this point that Birch's phone buzzed. Tanner didn't allow ringtones during any of his sessions. There was more than one small scratch upon the wall from where the soldier had confiscated and smashed devices. It didn't pay to ignore or defy the instructor's advice. Birch's expression was the soul of self-importance, as he scurried out of the room to answer the call - after giving his colleague another brief, conspiratorial look. Both men had mentioned to Ambler that he was now "part of the team." But, if he was, he felt like the new guy that they would not bring into their confidence because he wouldn't be staying around for too long.

As Birch took his call in the hallway outside Tanner recapped and tested the joe. Drilled him. Ambler rattled off addresses, put names to faces, and went through his prospective schedule upon landing at the Josi Marti International Airport. Afterwards, his gruff instructor offered up a hum and nod of appreciation.

"Good job."

For some reason Ambler found himself desiring the soldier's respect and approval. Birch may have fancied himself as David Stirling, but Tanner was Paddy Mayne. His words were worth more than a glowing *Daily Telegraph* review, or certainly a review in *The Guardian*.

When Birch returned, replete with knitted brow, he gave another revealing (yet vague) conspiratorial nod to an unmoved Tanner.

"Will you be fine to run the exercise without me?" Birch remarked, talking across Ambler.

"Yes."

The handler then turned to his new joe. Ambler couldn't quite be sure whether Birch uttered the words with an element of sympathy or sadism:

"We have received word from Vetrov's intermediary. You will be travelling to Cuba the day after tomorrow."

17.

After a few long seconds Ambler lifted his jaw from off the carpeted floor. He knew that the sentence would be coming, informing him of the date of his departure, but it still came as a shock. The news knocked the wind - and quips - out of him. Birch instructed his joe that he would be in touch soon, to square away certain arrangements and details. His old friend placed a hand on his shoulder, to perhaps steady the novelist, as it looked like his legs might give way at any moment.

Birch advised that, for now, Ambler should just concentrate on the task that Tanner was about to set him. He added that he would join them at the end of the exercise to assess his performance. Ambler wondered if the whole genesis of the operation was just a ruse for his friend to make him jump through hoops and play top dog. "The political is always a manifestation of the personal," one of the spy novelist's protagonists once postulated.

Birch departed, tapping away on his phone - contacting his wife, mistress or boss.

The stolid Tanner loomed large over his charge, his lantern jaw resembling a statue from Easter Island. Ambler noticed an L-shaped scar beneath his chin.

"We are going to play a bit of a game this afternoon. I call it the Fox and the Hounds. You will be taking the role of the fox. Your aim is to travel across London - and lose your pursuers. Put them off the scent. The trouble is, you will not know who your opponents are - unless you use your cunning and identify them. They may be travelling by foot or vehicle. Everyone may be a suspect. The lesson is not just to teach you how to lose a tail, but to do so without giving away that you are being followed. I shall brief you a little more and give you some tips, so the deck isn't entirely stacked against you. I should say though that whatever you think of out there, it's likely that the dogs have thought of it beforehand. This isn't their first hunt. You can walk or use public transport. You will have two hours to get from here to the Centre Point building, in Tottenham Court Road. Hopefully you will learn a thing or two, one of which is to always be alert. The service does not want to send you out into the field as a complete virgin. As virgins always get fucked, sooner or later," Tanner said, his face breaking out into a rare grin, as he enjoyed his own joke. He had regaled plenty of other joes with the comment over the years, but it never failed to amuse him.

As much as Tanner might assert that the exercise was just a formality, it was important for HR that they ticked the box of giving their joe some real "field training" before sending him off into the great unknown. Compliance Managers were the flavour of the month at the service. Should something happen to their man, who was also a borderline celebrity and a news headline, it was important that they cover themselves. It may have been a risk sending a virgin out into the night, but the risk would hopefully be worth the reward.

Tanner checked his watch and nodded. Pleased that he was on schedule. He was due to billet with one of his ex-wives after the exercise. The first, Pamela from Colchester, was a good cook. The second, Martina, was a lush and it was likely he would sleep in the marital bed again. He was genuinely torn.

But duty called.

"Give us ten minutes," the soldier said, over the phone. "I just need to debrief our boy a bit more - and then we'll be ready to play."

And you said it wasn't a game, Ambler thought to himself. Wanting to win.

Ambler was remarkably calm - or forced himself to be remarkably calm. A strategy began to form. *Let them think that I'm an amateur*, the spy novelist mused. He would walk to Centre Point. Ambler didn't enjoy public transport - or the public - at the best of times. Time would be on his side, if nothing else. Time and Mike Benson. Without being obvious, he would check car wing mirrors and shop windows for prospective hounds. His brain was alert. Sucking in everything. Separating the wheat from the chaff. He spotted a Ferrari, the same model as the one which had crashed into him all those months ago. Different number plates, however. Ambler was also on the alert for black cab drivers who could be hounds (the vehicles were used by MI6 as well as the Russians to pursue their quarry through the capital). A spook had recently told him how watchers had taken to using the ubiquitous delivery bike to blend in too. It was cheaper and greener, which pleased some. Constantly check for any conspicuous and repeat faces. Ambler performed one double-back loop just to show that he was trying and playing the game. But the team of watchers would be careful and coordinated, well-drilled in relation to merging into the crowd. The hounds would have a nose for their sport. *Also note inconspicuous figures.* London was full of colourful characters, who were, of course, interminably dull. The capital was a melting pot, one which seldom boiled over - despite the best efforts of the likes of BLM, Tommy Robinson, Antifa, the BNP and Sadiq Khan. Although in Knightsbridge (the only tube station with six consecutive consonants in its name), Ambler wasn't surprised to spot a bearded tramp in a tatty donkey jacket wolfing down a *Greggs* pasty. He was even less shocked to observe a Slavic beauty, wearing a skimpy dress that would make even an escort blush, sashay out of a Thai restaurant, carrying a snorting Boston terrier in her handbag. The theory was that a watcher could be anyone. But the vector was narrower. Ambler had encountered and interviewed plenty of "hounds" during his career. They used to be sour-faced ex-soldiers or former policemen, the kind that were not averse to a good baton charge. Nowadays, they were fresh-faced graduates. Despite the drive for more diverse recruitment, they were invariably white. Ambler remembered how one watcher asserted that "Climate change is the enemy now, not Russia or China," with a worrying lack of sarcasm.

He walked briskly, but not too briskly. There was time to take a circuitous route. He stopped off at a coffee shop, sitting with his back to the wall. Taking in any customers who came through the

119

door, or people who lingered on the opposite side of the street. The novelist noted faces, as clothes could easily be discarded and replaced. He drank a coffee and went to the toilet for a few minutes. Long enough for some of his suspected dogs to consider that he might have bolted. But he returned, to order a mineral water. A constant stream of customers entered and departed. Ambler had sympathy for the careworn Polish waitress, rushed off her feet. Overworked and underpaid. The crows' feet around her eyes were starting to resemble scars. Her smile and the soles of her shoes were starting to wear thin. Ambler offered up his own smile - and more importantly a ten-pound tip - as he left.

You can't take it with you.

Walking through the centre - but not necessarily the heart - of London reminded Ambler of how much he enjoyed being away from it all. From people. He felt the call of Greenwich again. His dream house, and the woman of his dreams. And how he turned things into a nightmare. The writer had no one else to blame. Ambler had been the author of his own demise. Lying and cheating.

"I think you were always going to get bored with me, be one of those men who trade their wives in for a younger mistress," Sara had said on the night she calmly and sadly asked him to leave. Her hands shook as she cradled a cup of milk-less tea (she had asked him to pick up some shopping before coming home but he forgot). "I hoped that you wouldn't be such a cliché. You're not, Daniel, in so many other ways... I used to love reading your books, but I can't anymore. I see too much of you in them, or the person you want to project into the world. But I know the real you. The callous and selfish you... I'm exhausted, tired of accusing myself that I did something wrong. I shouldn't feel guilty, but I do... Marriage is, or should be, something sacred. Or am I just being a naïve, Catholic girl? We are all attracted to Byron and think we can change or save him. But it's best we marry Keats... I need you to leave."

The cup shook more. Ambler was worried that the tea might even spill over and scald her hand.

DUTY CALLS

The fox entered a couple of busy shops and surveyed who might be following him. But he had no expectation of seeing any familiar faces or losing the hounds. Years ago, he may have been able to spot his pursuers by their earpieces. But over half the crowd seemed to be wearing earbuds, as they listened to music or took calls. Ambler was tempted to put on his own earphones and catch up with a few *Aspects of History* podcasts, hosted by Oliver Webb-Carter. The dogs often triangulated around their target, but they could be getting outside help. It was possible that his opponents were tapped into the CCTV network, which they utilised for other training exercises and real operations. It would make his task doubly difficult. But not impossible. Tanner hadn't mentioned that they were using CCTV. But spying is cheating and lying.

He fancied that Birch would like the idea of being all-seeing, through the legion of surveillance cameras in the capital. Left to his own devices, in the operation room, he would probably use the cameras to peer down the blouses of young women. Be a virtual stalker. God knows that he wouldn't be the only pervert in the service, though. They were as prevalent as prime ministers who had attended Oxford.

After stopping off at another coffee shop and going through the same ritual of sitting with his back to the wall, drinking and going to the toilet, Ambler decided to pop into a department store on Oxford St, to purchase a suit for his imminent trip. He should look good on his first day in his new job, regardless of the standard of his performance. The writer was also tempted to buy a Panama hat, to give himself an added air of authenticity. Or fake authenticity. He recalled a line from le Carré's *The Tailor of Panama*, which understandably gave the novelist pause: *"Everything in the world is true if you invent it hard enough and love the person it's for!"* As he travelled up the escalator, the fox nonchalantly turned around to survey the scene below. He recognised a hound, not through any talent of discerning indicators of interest, but because the beetle-browed figure had sat in on a couple of meetings when Ambler had visited MI6.

Ambler pretended not to notice the watcher. A lifetime of acting, or being, indifferent was bearing fruit. Or bearing more fruit.

Ambler continued to meander more than a Ronnie Corbett monologue. He veered off into Soho, which was ironically named after a hunting cry originating in the Tudor period, when the area was home to a different type of game. People spilled out onto the streets from the various louche and trendy bars. There were plenty of side streets and shops to attempt to disappear into. But, aided by the raft of CCTV cameras, his watchers could still easily be triangulating around him. The joe would wait to make his move.

He headed into Charlotte St, walking in the opposite direction to Centre Point, and turned into the small wine bar of *Bobo Social*. A regular sat outside, working his way through a coffee and cigarette, watching the world and short-skirted office girls go by. The establishment, which had dining space on the ground floor and a bar in the basement, was a popular venue for book launches. The decor was smart, the staff friendly and the wine list specially curated. Ambler popped in when he was in the area. He had met the owner, Mike Benson, through Marshal. Mike was Welsh, albeit his accent hinted at him being South African, from having worked there for many a year. He had also lived in Israel and France, before settling down in London. He worked hard and smart - but knew how to clock off too by raising a glass and laugh.

Thankfully, Mike was on site. The two men shook hands, albeit Ambler angled his back so that anyone outside couldn't witness the familiar greeting. He sat at the rear, ordered a beer and hung his jacket and new suit on the back of his chair. Doubtless the heat of Havana - and prospect of being watched by a Russian wet squad - would make him sweat, but right now Ambler was calm. A man with a plan.

"I need a small favour, Mike."

"Fire away," the Welshman replied, placing a cold bottle of beer on the table, along with a frosted glass.

"I've got a photographer following me. Or, worse, it's a fan. He's just lingering across the street, out of sight, at the moment. But he could well come in. I'm not in the mood to be bothered. Is there any way I can slip out the back way? I'll leave my jacket and shopping here so if they come in, they'll just think that I'm in the toilet. I can pick it up later, after a meeting I've got to go to."

"Sure. No problem. The price of fame, eh?"

"Aye. And they don't even give you any tax breaks for it. I'll duly finish my beer first, though. I'm not that desperate to escape."

The two men spoke briefly about their mutual friend, Marshal. They wondered if he might get engaged soon.

"I'm not sure which is the worst four letter word, marriage or divorce," Ambler remarked.

"Or which is the cheapest," Mike posed.

Ambler disappeared, but not to the toilet. He ventured up one more flight of stairs to reach the flat on the second floor. A window led out onto the roof, which he proceeded to clamber down from - via not the sturdiest ladder in the world - to reach an alleyway. Mike had assured him that the alley, after a dogleg turn, reached the main street. Ambler ran. Legs pumping. Tom Cruise-like. The little engine that could. Sweating the indifference out of him. Caring about evading the dogs, winning and making the operation a success.

Tanner stood at the foot of Centre Point, a face like thunder. Running a hand through his hair and rubbing his burgeoning stubble. Earlier in the afternoon he had yawned a few times and rolled his eyes, in response to the novelist's predictable moves, which his team of watchers reported back to him. *The fox would not escape the hounds*, Tanner thought confidently but not arrogantly.

But he had. The soldier shoved a torrent of expletives into the earpieces of his young team. Bollocking them. Repositioning them. They were on a training exercise too. They were green. *Or brown, like shit.* The snowflakes would think that Tanner was being that chiefest of sins - unfair. But every soldier needs a beasting at some point. Spying is soldiering. Spying isn't fair. Spying isn't a safe space.

"You're supposed to be the fucking professionals - and he should be the wanking amateur. What do you mean you can't see him? Have you got blood in your eyes still, from having just been pulled out of your mother's cunt?!"

"He's in the toilet still, I'm sure of it," Cameron, the team leader of the watchers, had feebly insisted, arguing that their target had spent time in the facilities of other establishments he had visited. Cameron Benn was the son of an old colleague. The apple hadn't fallen far from the tree. The father was a Rupert. The son was a Rupert. Shallow gene pools don't work, in families or in organisations. Cameron may have known his *Excel* from his *PowerPoint*, but he struggled to discern his arse from his elbow.

"I suggest that you go in there and check the toilets. I suspect that you'll find your career there rather than the target."

They liaised with their colleague, who was supporting them from an ops room and utilising the CCTV network. But nothing.

A few minutes later each member - of the team of "fucking headless chickens" - checked in with Tanner to report that they still did not have eyes on their quarry.

"I know you don't. Because I do," the veteran replied, staring at the sweat-glazed novelist strolling towards him, who was doing his best to appear insouciant whilst catching his breath.

The run had jarred Ambler's back a little, but it had been worth it. Just to witness Tanner's disgruntled scowl - and then his look of begrudging respect.

"Is it over?" the joe asked, knowing that the real work had not even started.

"Yes," Tanner replied, just about willing to concede that the spy novelist had won. "You're either a lucky bastard or a sly bastard. I'll happily take one or the other. Now, I was going to invite my sorry excuse for a team out for a drink, to celebrate. But they've pissed that opportunity up the wall. Never reward failure. They can spend their night writing up a report about how they're as useful as a eunuch in a brothel. I'll buy you a drink instead."

"I know a place," Ambler said, thinking about how he needed to pick up his jacket in Charlotte St.

Before they set off, however, a flustered Birch alighted from a black cab - paying a minimum tip and ensuring that he received a receipt to claim the money back on expenses.

One might have imagined that the handler would have been pleased for his joe, for having passed the exercise with flying colours. But a frown rather than smile flickered across his face (which Ambler had a growing suspicion had been botoxed recently). A piece of the agent died, upon hearing of his friend's success. Glossing over Ambler's achievement, he reminded his charge that there was still lots of work to be done. He needed to be fresh in the morning, for a final debrief, so he warned his joe about drinking too much down the pub. He knew how the rough-hewn ex-soldier could be a good and bad influence.

"Too much is still sometimes not enough," Tanner remarked, once they set off in the opposite direction to Birch, sounding even more world weary as his drinking companion.

18.

They were soon on their third or fourth bottle of beer in Charlotte Street. They christened each one with a clink, saying "cheers", before drinking. Mira, the general manager of the bar, sat them on a quiet table in the basement. She never quite knew whether to be worried, or impressed, by how much the writer could drink.

Ambler shifted a little uncomfortably in his seat again. The sprint to evade the hounds had aggravated his coccyx.

"Are you okay?" Tanner asked, in a rare gesture towards basic sympathy. Cold beer always helped thaw out the soldier's mood.

"I suffer from back pain every now and then. It's nothing," Ambler said casually, although he thought again how MI6 could repay him by tracking down the bastard who had run into him all those months ago. The author's lawyer could do the rest.

"I thought it might be that Birch put your back out. He can sometimes cause a pain in my wallet, as he seems to think he's above ever paying for a drink. You knew him during your university days, no? Was he a bit of a prick back then too?"

"Of course. It was Oxford. We believed we were the elite. Born to rule. Enlightened. Gold in our soul, as opposed to lead, like the plebs. Or non-Oxbridge graduates, as they're deemed by some. Unfortunately, plenty of people who attended Oxford, or even any university, still think that. I was doubtless a prick too, or at the very least a conceited shit. Birch's problem, or one of them, is that he is desperate for people to respect him, which is the reason, or one of them, why people don't respect him. He spent his adolescence - and beyond - trying to please his father. Tarquin Birch loomed large in his son's life. Simon was also eclipsed by some bright siblings. It was always expected, I think, that he should follow in his father's footsteps and join the service. I met his father a few times. He was incredibly vain and racist, even for a Yorkshireman. He would have been a Tory, or Labour, peer if he lived longer. "I want to make my mark," Simon has often said to me, over the years. But I fear that he may just create a vague stain somewhere. But if we pull this off - and the treasure is as valuable as he hopes - then he may well get his wish and make his mark."

"And do you trust your old friend?"

"I trust him more than any Russian agent, if that's an answer."

"You are a quick study. You're going to be okay. You'll go to Cuba and be back before you can even get a tan. You'll be in like Flynn. They had some analysts do a deep dive, or as deep as they could, on Rybin. Neither he nor his associates are due to travel to Havana. I guess I should try and read one of your bloody books, while you're away. Can you recommend any?"

"I'll get you a copy of *The Silent Type*. The protagonist is an ex-soldier. He's an ornery bastard, rather than a prick or conceited shit. You'd like him. It's also got a twist that few readers see coming. The villain of the piece isn't always the person you expect."

Footsteps could be heard on the stairs as Mira led a few customers into the basement. America tourists. Their voices as loud as their outfits. It was time for the servicemen to stop talking shop.

"All's well that will end well," Tanner said, his voice less gruff, as the two men clinked their bottles in one more toast

Havana.

The air rippled with heat over dilapidated buildings. Russia had come a long way in a short time. Cuba had come a short way in a long time. The Russian removed his Panama hat and mopped his corrugated brow. Despite spending plenty of time in Tel Aviv, Istanbul and Tehran over the past two decades he did not take to the dirty heat of the city. Russians often romanticised their suffering, but Cuba seemed to revel in its squalor.

He sat out on the balcony of his hotel suite. He had been tempted to book out the entire floor, for privacy and quietude, but the foreigner did not want to draw too much attention to himself. He wanted to come and go, unnoticed.

Vintage cars spluttered along the sun-baked road below. He could taste the salt in the air from the sea. Mewling children could be heard, along with the distant sound of drums and singing (unfortunately not distant enough, for the drear Russian). A half-finished plate of specially ordered devilled kidneys, along with chopped eel, garlic and raw onions, drizzled over with a béarnaise sauce, sat on the polished marble-topped table in front of him. He had been all over the world, but no one could cook fried eel with garlic and onion like his grandmother. The complimentary bottle of rum had been swapped out for a bottle of expensive vodka. The fastidious, sixty-something examined his manicured fingernails, before crushing an insect beneath his thumb (one could imagine him as a child, or man, impassively pulling the legs of spiders).

Flies began to infest the air. His irritation was tempered by the thought that they would soon feast on the Englishman's rotting corpse. His mouth tightened and his hand bunched into a fist when he thought of the writer. His initial preference had been to travel to London to deal with him. He wanted to look over a property he had recently purchased there and be fitted for some new suits. But the powers that be would not sanction another killing in London. One of the Russian's lieutenant's, Yuri Tasarov, was at Vetrov's villa now. Preparing for the novelist's arrival.

Despite his wealth and trips to warmer climes, the Russian possessed fewer summer suits than one might have imagined. But he wore one now. A dull beige. Pronounced seams on the trousers. The smell of cigar smoke from a balcony below drifted up and made his beak of a nose twitch. Short, iron-grey hair. Pitted skin (rumour had it that he wore make-up on special occasions). A cruel, letterbox mouth - accustomed to issuing kill orders - was as unwavering as the rest of his face. It was an expression, hewn from stone, unused to compromise or whimsy. The Russian was a man who was perpetually taking care of business. The chess player liked to, or needed to, think several moves ahead. It seemed that the gulls at MI6 only thought one move ahead. Their eyes on the prize had blinded them to the truth.

He checked his watch. A *Patek Philippe*. Worth six figures. All his watches ran five minutes fast. He hated being late. He also hated those who were tardy. His disciplinarian father had drilled into him, as a child, the importance of being on time. As was his habit, the Russian tapped his index finger on the glass two times before the watch disappeared beneath the silk cuffs of his shirt. Was the small, frequent ritual borne out of superstition? He had initially started tapping his watch faces after purchasing his first expensive timepiece, a diamond encrusted *Cartier*. The watch was a symbol and reminder of how far he had come. He had grown used to the finer things in life over the past couple of decades. Before then, he had been familiar with the less finer things in life.

The Russian suppressed a yawn, from jetlag. The flight had been long. Thankfully he had been able to purchase the seat next to him so he could not be disturbed. He wanted to be free from prying eyes or "chit-chat". He found it difficult to sleep on airplanes. He had never been one to read novels or watch inane American movies. Tiredness began to weigh on his shoulders and eyelids, but it would have been weakness to submit or display his fatigue. There was work to be done, plans to be finalised. A rare, faint smile - blink and you would have missed it - played on the Russian's lips as he thought how Yuri would be currently transforming Vetrov's wine cellar into a make-shift interrogation room. Torture chamber.

"Eat something when you get home. Have a whisky. Settle your stomach and settle your nerves. Get plenty of sleep. We have one last debrief tomorrow," Tanner had ordered at the end of their drinks, or rather his tone had softened towards the new joe. It seemed more like he was providing friendly advice.

Ambler emailed his editor on the way home, to confirm he would be travelling to Havana for a few days. Powell replied with some suggestions regarding restaurants and places of interest to visit. He also mentioned how Tamara Fallon had requested that the author tweet about his trip. Ambler didn't dignify that part of the email with a response.

He sent a message to Marshal, saying that he would meet and pay him tomorrow. If Ambler died, he did not want to go to the next life owing money to anyone in this one, particularly Marshal.

Give a cock to Alcibiades.

Ambler also needed to see Sara, whether it would be for the last time or not. He needed a slight ruse. He messaged her that a publisher had sent him a box of new books which he thought she might like. He was about to go on a trip. Could he bring them over later? There was a slight delay before she replied but Sara said thank you - and Ambler was welcome to bring the books over at five o'clock. But he needed to be on time as she was going out at six. Ambler popped into the bookshop on Kensington High St and purchased several new releases from the major publisher. Somehow not seeing Sara before he flew off into the unknown would be tantamount to not receiving the last rites. The Catholic had collected other sacraments, like marking off numbers on a bingo card. His catechism teacher, as a boy, had defined sacraments as outward signs of inward grace. But how much grace had he received? Next to none. But, then again, how much grace had he put out into the world? Perhaps less than none. But who had? Sara.

Kitty beckoned the regular in, as he passed by the pub. Perhaps the barmaid was keen to ask after Marshal. He smiled back but shook his head.

Ambler had utilised his training on the way home, checking for any Range Rovers, black cabs or potential FSB agents. There were none. All would be well, he told himself. Half-convincingly. Or a smidgeon over half.

As Ambler put his key into the door of his flat his phone vibrated with a couple of texts from Samantha. Part of him still wanted to have sex with her. He was only human, or a man, after all. He just didn't want to hear about the latest fusion restaurant to open in New York, or the best "on trend" tech stock to invest in. The first message from the American was passive aggressive. The second was just aggressive. Ambler was either too tired or distracted to reply.

He decided to take Tanner's advice. The joe cooked himself a simple meal, had a whisky and listened to some music, before drifting off to sleep.

"I'll wait on God's creation
Just to show her a man can change."

He had an important day, tomorrow. And the day after that would be even more significant. Longer too.

19.

Ambler received a message from his agent as he walked towards the safe house in Knightsbridge. Ponsonby, who heard he was travelling to Cuba from Tim Powell, asked if he wanted to write a travel piece for one of the major newspapers whilst there. The agent sent a list of names for his author to pitch a feature to. The agent would also sort payment and receive a twenty percent commission for his enterprise and effort. Did anyone else know he was Havana-bound? The spy novelist fancied that his mission was becoming less clandestine by the hour, although he could claim that such things were all useful for his cover. The joe was building up his legend. *Some legend*, he wryly thought.

The debrief went well. Ambler displayed impressive recall in relation to putting names to faces and reeling off contacts, addresses and instructions. They went through the plan again. And then again. Tanner led the meeting. Birch seemed engrossed with his phone and merely offered up occasional pearls of wisdom, as well as reminding Ambler about the terms of the agreement in the document he signed. They went through procedure and protocol one last time about what should happen when he landed in Havana - and reassured their man that nothing would go awry.

"No wonder he was top of his class at university," Tanner commented, knowing that he would irritate his colleague by saying so.

Birch ignored the jibe and went on to re-lecture Ambler on how he should deal with their prize asset, once ensconced at the villa.

"Humour him. Indulge him… And you will win him over."

The joe thought how perhaps he had been humoured and indulged and won over. Ambler knew he was being played, to some extent, but he was willing to play along.

"You are ready," Tanner said, towards the close of their session. The recruit had aced his tests, but how well could he perform out of the classroom and in the field? Time would soon tell. As one of his instructors in Hereford, during SAS selection, had always said, "Diamonds are created through pressure."

"Thank you, Daniel. Your country thanks you too," Birch added, as all three men around the table got to their feet. Somehow it came across, though, that Ambler should be thanking his handler for the opportunity to make a difference and do something meaningful with his life.

Tanner shook his hand - less firmly than when they had first been introduced. But less meant more. Birch's handshake was akin to clasping a wet haddock. Ambler fancied that his friend resembled an officer in the Great War, wishing a nameless Tommy well, before the poor soul went over the top.

The two men met in the *American Bar* at *The Stafford Hotel*. The drinks were expensive, but Ambler liked the aesthetic and service. He had fond memories of picking up women there too. Both men angled themselves so they're backs were to the wall and they could keep an eye on who was walking in. The bar had been a haunt for American fighter pilots during the Second World War. Pictures and paraphernalia adorned the walls. Phalanxes of multi-coloured baseball caps hung from the ceiling, containing images of propellers, airplanes and animal insignias. Spirit bottles and gleaming crystal glasses furnished the dark wood bar. Too many men were drinking cocktails containing olives, in Cosmopolitan glasses, but so be it. Women power-dressed but were not averse to simpering. A hubbub of American accents could be heard but thankfully not too many. Cigar smoke shuffled in from where patrons smoked outside. The music was blandly ambient, but unobtrusive. It was the calm before the storm of the evening rush.

"Are you sure this is not too much?" Marshal said, after Ambler passed over the thick brown envelope of cash. The ex-para liked to avoid both the Taliban and taxman.

"I'm more worried about it not being enough. I'm sorry, again, about all the unpleasantness the other night. It's become an affair to remember, for all the wrong reasons."

Marshal shrugged and replied:

"Life wouldn't be life without a bit of unpleasantness every now and then. Let me know if ever the husband puts his head above the parapet. I'd have no problem being unpleasant to him again."

Ambler pictured Connor Mason. In the carpark he had experienced a paralysing sense of fear, but now he felt twinges of shame. The author wanted to cringe rather than run for cover at the memory. If he couldn't deal with the thought of Connor Mason, then he wouldn't be able to even board the plane and deal with the thought of Viktor Rybin or Vetrov.

God - and he thought he had trouble making a leap of faith in being a Catholic. Making a leap of faith into the crucible of Havana was not without its doubts as well. Ambler teasingly thought, what was the worst that could happen? His capture or death would at least be good for publicity and book sales, but there were understandably lots of things in the "con", as opposed to "pro" column, concerning that scenario.

"So where are you heading off to now? Back home, to pack?" Marshal asked.

"I'm going to see Sara."

The soldier arched an eyebrow. The rest of his expression, or lack of expression, could have been interpreted in a myriad of ways. Suggestive. Censorious. Amused.

Ambler thought how he wanted to tell Sara how he felt about her. It would help, first, if he knew what he felt. All he knew was that he felt too much. He imagined the different reactions on her face if he bared what was left of his ragged heart. He was familiar with most, if not all, of his ex-wife's expressions, including those which were less kind and less comely. He wondered how much he could or should tell her. The Official Secrets Act should not get in the way of true love. It was likely that the novelist would be lost for words when he sat down in front of her.

Marshal's attention was briefly drawn towards a couple of half-cut Americans, who were clicking their fingers at a young, Italian waiter. The soldier looked like he was on the cusp of marching over to the brash wasps, snapping off the offending fingers like twigs and stuffing them down their gullets. On another table Ambler saw an MP placing a flabby hand on the thigh of the young woman he was sharing a bottle of champagne with (doubtless on expenses). The blonde was probably a member of his staff rather than his wife, given the affection he was displaying. Ambler couldn't remember which party he was from - and didn't much care either.

Silence hung in the air, more like a bat than hummingbird, until Ambler spoke again:

"I know. You don't have to say anything. I'm unsure about what I'm going to tell Sara too. But I'm going to conveniently change the subject. I'm no advertisement for marriage, or divorce, of course - but will you be proposing to Grace in the near future?"

It was now Marshal's turn to let silence hang in the air. He had asked the same question of himself, at more than one juncture, during the past year. He couldn't love Grace more. Like Kierkegaard, in relation to his fiancé Regina Olsen, Marshal had told himself - "Marry her or do not marry at all." He was content at the moment. Marriage could only change that, he feared. The soldier knew so few souls, if any, who were happily married. Some were happily divorced, however.

"I wish that I had an answer for you - and myself."

They ordered another round of beers, but they seemed only half present as they engaged with one another. Ambler dwelled upon Sara and Havana. Marshal thought of Grace. Even alcohol couldn't wash away the air of melancholy.

It was time to go. The clock was ticking, especially for Ambler. The two men shared a look (whether consoling, wry or resigned), took a breath and got to their feet. Ambler insisted on settling the bill. Although he had paid Marshal, he still felt like he was in his debt. For past or future services rendered. The driver went to shake his client's hand but, in a rare show of emotion, Ambler hugged Marshal - as if he might never see him again. The usually impassive soldier appeared a mite uncomfortable.

Whilst Ambler looked to flag down a cab to take him to Greenwich, he received another text from Samantha. The message lacked photos and, thank God, emojis this time. She wrote several lines, chiding her part-time lover and hinting at what he was missing out on. At the end she declared that he "had changed".

Aye, and hopefully for the better, Ambler judged.

20.

The carrier bags (not from *Waterstone's*) containing the books cut into his fingers as Ambler got out of the cab in Greenwich. The slight discomfort didn't quite generate enough Dostoyevskian suffering to expatiate his sins. He stood outside the house, morbidly thinking if he would ever see it again. But then thankfully laughed out loud. The author's sense of morbidity - and humour – continued. He wondered, should he never come back, whether Sara would wear black after the funeral too, like a widow. If he came back wounded or traumatised, would she nurse him back to health? Ambler didn't care if the world saw him as a hero or not, even for the sake of book sales, but he did want Sara to think more of him. The irony would be that all would run smoothly, even dully, concerning *Operation Pancho Villa*. MI6 would airbrush him out of the story or deny his involvement. He was just "a glorified mule," as Tanner explained. Or, as Ambler thought at the time, he was *an ass*.

Sara thanked her ex-husband for the books and invited him in, with the caveat that she would need to leave for dinner within the hour. Ambler followed Sara into the kitchen, doing his best (but failing) not to stare at her figure in a navy-blue pencil skirt, hemline above the knee, and pearl-coloured silk blouse. Her hair hung down, glossy. Her skin glowed. Ambler told himself she was glowing from her tan, rather than from any date she might be about to go on. He noticed how her nails were freshly painted. She always painted her nails before a date with Ambler, when they were courting. Beauty can be a source of pain rather than inspiration if you are unable to possess it. But Sara wouldn't want him to be jealous right now. He didn't want to be jealous right now.

She apologised for having to answer a message on her phone, explaining that it was work related. She grinned when typing. An indicator of interest, if ever there was one. How many times had

Ambler explained to his wife that he was texting because of a work issue when he was replying to a mistress?

As usual, Sara was doing more than one thing at a time - tidying, attending to her guest, working on the laptop, brushing her hair. It was exhausting, just watching her. Ambler wanted her to sit down, be still, hear his last confession. He told her that he would be travelling to Cuba for a few days, for a research trip. But... And that was when Sara took a call and darted out of the kitchen, her heels rhythmically clicking across the hardwood floor. Yet, even if all the stars aligned, Ambler could convince himself that it was the wrong place and the wrong time to unburden his heart. She had moved on - and he had seemingly moved on. He wasn't a young man anymore, a Romeo who was able to prove himself by scaling up to a balcony to reach his Juliet. There was also the inconvenient truth. It was entirely possible that after confessing his feelings and revealing he was a spy, about to save the world, Sara would still reject him. It would be the final nail in the coffin. He thought how he needed to be friends with the woman who he still loved. Second best would be good enough, if it meant not betting everything on red and it landed on black. *There are no happy endings.*

Sara returned to find Ambler staring sullenly, or sorrowfully, into space. It looked like someone had told him that he had a month left to live.

"You seem like you are on another planet, or perhaps you're already in Havana. A penny, or some pesos, for your thoughts?" she said, prettily tucking her hair behind her ear. She was wearing new earrings. Sara preferred the ones Ambler had bought her, for their wedding anniversary a few years back, but she thought it would be inappropriate to wear them on her date.

"Oh, I'm not sure they're worth that much. I'm just thinking about what my next book project should be," Ambler replied. He was a good liar. Too good.

"We both know that you should be writing a biography of Turgenev."

"But knowing and doing are two different things. I suspect I'll just follow the money, rather than my heart. It'll be easy money. Once you think of a twist for a spy thriller then every else slots into place."

"At least you are getting a nice research trip out of writing the novel. I never thought that Cuba would be on your bucket list as a place to travel to, though."

"I'm sure that the communists there will welcome me with open arms. Or firearms."

Ambler wanted to add how he was really travelling to Havana to see a former Russian oligarch. Yevgeny Vetrov had taken more than thirty pieces of silver when betraying his beliefs, as the good soviet turned into a good capitalist. Rather, he had taken a majority shareholding in a once state owned steel foundry. The author remembered having dinner with the oligarch several years ago. Vetrov was half-drunk and wholly pleased with himself - a fervent convert to the capitalist system. All he needed was a copy of *Atlas Shrugged* tucked under his arm, Ambler had thought.

"You know what I have learnt, Daniel? Life can and should be reduced to numbers," the porcine Russian pronounced, swaying in his chair a little, his fleshy hand cradling an expensive, aromatic cognac. "Procure a mistress half your age. Have twice as much money in the bank after every five-year cycle. Five-year cycle, mind you, not five-year plan, eh? Keep enough cash in the house so that you have enough money to bribe anyone daring to crash through the door. You see what I mean? We can reduce everything to numbers. A man's soul can be bought. It's just the price tags that are different for each person… Take this cognac I am drinking. It's ten thousand dollars a bottle, I believe. One glass will cost as much as what one of the waiters here will earn in a month, including tips. Is this immoral? No, it's just numbers. Value is value. Worth is worth. Money is money. We must deal with the world as it is, not as how we would like it to be," Vetrov pontificated, pointing a podgy finger at his dinner companion. "I didn't make the rules. I'm just trying to win the game. And even if I win, if I've not already won, what will I be? At best, I will be a small cog within a bigger set of wheels, or I am just one tooth on a small cog within a greater machine… Either God has a plan for everyone, and we must resign ourselves to our fate. Or God is an absent landlord - and there is no plan. Nothing matters. Nothing has real value. Ach, I'm drinking and talking too much."

Ambler very much agreed with his last point.

He wondered if Vetrov would agree with his former self now, or would his illness inspire a deathbed conversion? Having been exiled by Putin, a larger cog in the machine, he now had less of his wealth to give away. Ambler didn't know if that would make things easier or harder for the convert to capitalism.

"Are you okay, Daniel?" Sara asked, as Ambler appeared to be in a world of his own again. A lonely world.

"Yes, sorry, I'm fine," he replied, with a faltering smile.

"You look tired. You should catch up on some sleep."

Ambler's faltering smile bolstered itself, as he remembered Tanner talking down the phone to his team after the exercise. Berating them, after one of the watchers asked if he could be excused for the evening to catch up on some sleep.

"Spies don't sleep. Spies don't have nights off. Spies don't exist, so how are they supposed to have fucking duvet days? If you're not feeling constantly tired and weary, then you're in the wrong profession. Even if you were successful during the exercise, which God and more importantly I know you weren't, you still wouldn't deserve a good night's kip. You failed, like a Muslim getting caught eating a bacon sandwich. Own your tit-wank mistakes, as well as any triumphs. Not even your father - and all the freemasons under the sun - would be able to save you and wash the smell of shit off should the training exercise have been a real op. Don't fucking call me again tonight, unless it's to tell me you've got AIDS," Tanner ranted, seemingly apoplectic, before hanging up the phone and boyishly grinning.

Ambler turned to his ex-wife replied:

"I'll sleep enough in the next life."

21.

"He's on the plane?" Boyd Hamilton asked, whilst perusing the wine menu of the Sardinian restaurant in Mayfair. An amber wall lamp glowed over their polished walnut table, pristine cotton napkins and gleaming cutlery.

"He's on the plane," Birch replied, assuredly, having just sat down. He noticed how his boss' index finger was over halfway down the page, way past the house wines. They were indeed having a celebratory lunch, the agent surmised. Both men were immaculately attired. The senior operative had even treated himself to a shave at Trumpers, although that may have partly been because he was due to have dinner with his mistress that evening.

"Well, our carrier pigeon has already gone further than others might have done, in his position. You did well, persuading and prepping him in such a short space of time. The old school ties are the ties that bind, it seems. Should all go according to plan, and our treasure is worthy of the name, you will receive a commendation at the very least." Birch was aware that his boss was laying more groundwork for harvesting the lion's share of credit for the successful operation. But Birch was happy for Hamilton to reap the rewards and earn a promotion. If he did, there would be a vacancy in the department for a rising star, one that his predecessor could trust.

"I could not have done it without you, sir. Despite my seniority in the department, you have taught me that I still have a lot to learn. This old dog still welcomes new tricks."

"Indeed. Now, do we have someone posted at the airport to confirm his arrival and to verify that he is being collected by Vetrov's driver?"

"Unfortunately not. Our resources in Havana are not what they used to be. One of our men stationed there is on paternity leave. The other has reported in sick. Incapacitated, with stomach cramps. He has only just come back from issues relating to mental health, apparently. We cannot trust any junior personnel available. They are wet behind the ears and do not possess the requisite clearance."

"Hmm," Hamilton replied, still contemplating the menu. "So, our new joe is on his own, for all intents and purposes?"

The corner of Hamilton's mouth twitched, twice. Did he feel a twinge of guilt or regret? Should they have alerted their American cousins to *Operation Pancho Villa* then they would have sufficient manpower and resources at their disposal. They could have eyes on the ground and eyes in the sky, in the form of satellite coverage. The British rightly believed that the quality of their personnel and intelligence were second to none, but the Yanks provided materiel and muscle - although the CIA couldn't exactly trumpet any great track record in Cuba. The Bay of Pigs was a pig's ear of an operation. Ill-conceived and ill-executed. He seemed to have a vague memory that the failed invasion had the codename of *Operation Zapata*. Hamilton tempered any sense of regret. The Americans would have wanted a seat around the table concerning his operation. *His* seat. Boyd Hamilton, soon to be perhaps *Sir* Boyd Hamilton (maybe one day even *Lord* Hamilton of Esher) had no desire to be Montgomery to someone else's Eisenhower. He even knew his opposite number, one Bradley Johnson, at Langley. He thought he was Allen Dulles recast, but really he was a vulgarian, creating dragons to slay to win favour with the Republican Party. No, his judgement had been sound. The mission would be a success. Again, Hamilton internally salivated at the intelligence they were about to obtain. Vetrov could well give them compromising video footage of the statesman-like Rybin rogering a child. Had "Rasputin" been caught, quite literally, with his pants down? Or, even worse for Rybin, had Vetrov gathered evidence of his bête noire with his hand in the cookie jar? Stealing from the kleptocratic state was one thing, but had the Russian committed the cardinal sin of embezzling funds from Putin? The state coffers and Putin's bank account could be considered one and the same thing, of course.

"Yes, but as a result there are few that are aware of *Operation Pancho Villa*. Ambler will arrive and depart without any fanfare. Small is beautiful, as they say."

"Indeed. So be it. Do we know what happened to the real Pancho Villa, by the way? I can't imagine that there are too many happy endings for Mexican revolutionaries."

"He was assassinated. It was one of the first assassinations involving dumdum bullets, I believe."

"Not the best omen for our joe, admittedly, but we cannot afford to be superstitious in our profession. Now, it seems that Tanner is unable to join us."

"Yes, he has a meeting he needs to attend."

"A shame," Hamilton said, lying. Barely disguising his lack of disappointment. The officer class around the table did not lament the former squaddie's absence. Hamilton appreciated having Tanner on the same team, but he did not wish to cultivate any conviviality between them. They were chalk and cheese. Hamilton wondered if Sardinia was a civilised enough island to serve port with any cheese board.

"One piece of news, which I received this morning. It turns out that Sergei Shunin is not in the country. We have confirmed sightings of him still present in Moscow, although the latest intelligence report has him travelling to Sheremetyevo airport."

"Let us hope that he is not boarding a flight to Cuba," Hamilton remarked, half-jokingly, as he decided on having the fried octopus with lemongrass and capers, to be followed by the veal.

Birch thought to himself that he should double-check to find out. But after lunch.

143

22.

Havana.

Ambler stepped off the plane, clad in his new but now slightly crumpled linen suit. A wave of dirty warmth struck him, as tangibly as a fist to the face - albeit the softest of punches. He squinted as he took in a burning blue sky, marked with a smattering of wispy clouds, seemingly melting in the heat like strips of lard melting in a pan. *Jose Marti International Airport*, named after the poet and revolutionary. There were worse poets and revolutionaries. Hordes of them. Ambler recalled a line Marti had composed, which he had glanced at in a feature contained in the in-flight magazine. A photograph accompanied the article. The Cuban resembled a gaunt Nietzsche.

"I am good, and as a good man
I will die facing the sun."

Through the shimmering air Ambler took in the patches of yellowing grass, sun-bleached plaster and plastic, scorched tarmac, toy-like planes in the distance and the far from impressive terminal. There were lots of Hawaiian shirts on display. Too many. Hands were raised, akin to Nazi salutes, from scores of people lifting their phones up and taking photographs. Instead of the smell of spiced rum and expensive cigars, his nostrils caught the whiff of aviation fuel, along with the florid fragrance of the stewardess' perfume. Ambler was too busy being relieved, to have landed safely and completed the first part of the operation, to know if he was overwhelmed or underwhelmed by the sight in front of him.

The flight was as uneventful as any other. Out of a kernel of spite, or a dedication to fiscal responsibility and giving taxpayers value for money, Birch had insisted that the service could only reimburse Ambler for the cost of a "Premium Economy" seat. For the sake of his back - and digestion - the novelist used his credit card, rather than any modicum of celebrity, to secure an upgrade to First Class.

He was looked after by Kim, as Asiatic-looking stewardess with a neat black bob, winsome expression and sweet nature. She displayed some indicators of interest, as did he.

"My job gives me a chance to see the world. I post photos of my meals and the places I visit on my Instagram page. I've got over two thousand followers. It's crazy!" Kim explained, torn whether to show him some of the photographs, which often featured the stewardess in outfits which left little, or a lot, to the imagination. Kim was known to take the contact details of those in First Class, but never in Economy.

Ambler feigned interest, saying that he admired her spirit of adventure.

Time was, in the past, the priapic author would have asked for her number. But the joe had enough numbers to memorise at present and didn't need the distraction.

The flight was nearly ten hours. Ambler tried to read - but failed. He tried to sleep - but there was a proverbial pea the size of a bowling ball beneath his seat-cum-bed. In an effort, which the writer thought was beyond him, he resisted the temptation of drinking his way through most of the flight. The mission loomed large in his mind, rather than the charms of the buxom stewardess. He went through the plan, again. And again. He started to compose some lines in his head, as if he were writing dialogue for a novel, which he would use to flatter his host and win his trust. Win the treasure. Vetrov's emissary had explained how the Russian was too sick to meet his guest at the airport - but that he would dispatch his driver to collect him. Ambler also thought how he would accept any invitation to ghost write the oligarch's life story if it meant completing the mission. The author could also use the money to fund his biography of Turgenev. Something good could come out of the operation, other than potentially saving the world - or, at the very least, Ukraine, Ambler wryly thought.

In between watching a couple of memorably forgettable movies, Ambler morbidly and playfully put together a setlist of songs he would like played at his funeral. There were plenty which made the longlist, but a pencilled in shortlist consisted of *Girl From the Red River Shore*, *The Philosopher's Stone* by Van Morrison and something plaintive by Willie Nelson. He pictured Sara crying - but smiling fondly at times too as she listened to the elegiac and revealing lyrics. He typed out a text afterwards to his wife, or ex-wife, confessing how he still loved her:

"...I'm doing something now that will hopefully atone for my sins, but not all of them. No one can atone for all their sins. That's a fool's errand. But I'm so sorry for everything. Perhaps even more than God, I need you to forgive me."

Ambler laughed at himself, however, and deleted the message before he could send it. The spy, who was travelling a third of the way around the world to potentially put himself in harm's way for Queen and country, was still as cowardly as the next man. As awful as the next man. Sara would probably have just dismissed his uncharacteristic declaration - and put it down to him being drunk - if he sent the words off into the ether. Nothing would change. Ambler would remain as damned as the next man. The decree nisi still stood.

Occasionally the novelist was amused by the conversation emanating from a young couple sitting nearby. Originally from Bristol, they now, thanks to an inheritance, lived in Hackney. But the nicer part. They dare not say the "whiter part," but that's what they meant. The girlfriend (Miranda) worked in HR, the boyfriend (Colin) in IT support. Colin wanted to lay flowers at Castro's grave and have his photo taken next to Che Guevara's statue. "I feel like I'm on a pilgrimage." Miranda was keen to have her photo taken on a beach, with a cocktail in her hand, to make her friends back home jealous. They looked forward to visiting a tobacco farm and meeting the "natives". "I want to see the real Cuba," Miranda enthused, clinging to her guidebook in one hand and her iPad, with several *Sex and the City* episodes downloaded on it, in the other. "You cannot buy the kind of experiences that we are paying for," Colin added, without irony.

As the plane descended Ambler caught glimpses of the make-up of the island. From a distance, the landscape teemed with beauty. Coral reefs, as white as Kim's teeth. Mountains, swathed in mist and carpeted with lush forests. Farmlands and wetlands. Ramshackle villages, with ribbons of silver smoke purring upwards, populated by warm-hearted locals, as well as drunks, wife-beaters and racists. Rugged yet attractive rock and cave formations. Shining, sandy beaches, like lacework on the hem of a colourful dress. Foaming, frothing waterfalls. It might indeed be worth setting a book in Cuba. Or at least part of one. He idly thought of some of the hotspots that his editor and Sara recommended he should visit. There was the Hemingway Museum (Ambler thought him an overrated writer and human being, which was not to say he wasn't a remarkable writer and human being). Maria urged him to visit the Basilica del Cobre, an old Catholic church. Any divine intervention would be welcome, to help him complete *Operation Pancho Villa*. God had long since taken an interest in Daniel Ambler (and vice-versa), the joe suspected, though. *La Guarida* - with its fish and chicken dishes - would be worth visiting, however.

Cuba had it all, he mused, aside from a functioning democracy (which, admittedly, didn't seem a system of government that was altogether highly prized nowadays). But they did have, according to Colin, "a socialist paradise". Ambler smiled as he recalled a quote, by J. K. Galbraith. *"Under capitalism, man exploits man. Under Communism, it's just the opposite."*

Yuri Tasarov informed his paymaster that the plane had touched down on time. Dmitri had also arrived at the airport, to collect the Englishman. Although it was welcome news, one wouldn't have known it given Yuri's dour, monotone voice. Muscles bulged beneath the ex-soldier's suit. Those with a trained eye might have noticed a handgun bulge beneath his jacket too.

The calm, stoic Russian nodded in reply. He checked his watch and tapped it two times. All was running according to plan. The plastic sheeting had been laid out down in the wine cellar, out of a small courtesy to their host, in preparation for their guest.

Like clockwork.

The wealthy, powerful Russian ran a ringed hand through his iron-grey hair and stared out through the window of Yevgeny Vetrov's villa. A few leaves, resembling scabs, lay upon the swimming pool. A faint smell of chlorine entered his nostrils. They would need more cleaning products downstairs, before the day was done, he fancied.

The Russian permitted himself another smile. He had read an interview with the novelist, when researching his target. The Englishman had said, "Even when we have the all-powerful Amazon algorithm on their side, authors seldom change the world." Such was the beauty of the plan that the Russian had executed, he had given Ambler hope - the thought that he was a good man, about to make a difference - so that he could take that away from him too. It is easy to turn an idealist into a cynic. Life will do that as par for the course, the worldly Russian believed. But to turn a cynic back into an idealist. Now that is something special. It was just a shame that the Englishman was divorced - and childless. The Russian knew all too well how families can make a man vulnerable, although he had seen more than one husband choose his wealth over his wife when push came to shove. The plan did not extend to drawing the former Mrs Ambler into his web, however. So be it.

Due to the nature of his short stay - and for expediency's sake - Ambler only had a carry-on bag. He did not need to suffer the wait and rigmarole of lingering next to the baggage carousel. He went through passport control remarkably quickly too. When he mentioned he was a writer, researching a novel, to the plump, lazy-eyed passport officer at the desk he was met with a distinct lack of interest or intrigue. Ambler hoped that he would be able to leave the island, as easily as he had entered it.

148

DUTY CALLS

He had to travel the length of the airport to reach the taxi ranks, where he was informed his driver would be waiting, to take him to Vetrov's villa. The air conditioning was on, but barely. As well as music from the Bueno Vista Social Club being played on a loop, he was greeted with another blast of heat, accompanied by bustling, babbling clumps of people. Tourists and locals combined. Airport staff, with drooping faces and drooping moustaches. Fellow travellers brushed past him. The joe could easily be pricked with a ricin-tipped umbrella or fountain pen, and he wouldn't even notice. Ambler told himself to remember his training and covertly surveyed the scene, for any watchers. But his brain felt frazzled. Fried. The smell of bleach and body odour ousted other competing aromas. The heat was as oppressive as the Chinese Communist Party. Sweat dripped into - and stung - his tired eyes. He could taste the salt on his top lip - and felt his shirt begin to stick to his aching back. It was so hot, Ambler was even tempted to undo a second button on his shirt. But, thankfully, he didn't give way to temptation. An Englishman abroad must remain an Englishman.

It was late afternoon, or early evening, but it resembled midday. Despite being more overpriced than French cuisine, Ambler purchased a bottle of water from a small shop, which also stocked a worrying range of vibrators made to resemble Cuban cigars. A small group of salsa dancers performed in the corner, their gaunt faces slick with perspiration. A couple seemed about to drop from exhaustion, as if they were a brace of extras from the film, *They Don't Shoot Horses, Do They?* Ambler was also taken back by the sheer volume of posters and advertising hoardings on display, promoting shops and nightclubs. He was assaulted by slogans, colours and special offers - although he rightly mused that there were worse ways of being assaulted, thinking back to events in the carpark with Connor Mason. One nightclub, *The Crimson Flamingo*, advertised its Afro-Cuban house band, a Phil Collins tribute act - *Another Day In Paradise*. Another advertisement promoted an "Ecotourism" company. Its slogan was *"Take a hike."* Ambler agreed.

As surely as cancer will get you in the end, Ambler thought how capitalism was coming to Cuba, when he took in the shiny new shop selling all manner of Fidel Castro paraphernalia: fans, nightshirts, tea towels, tankinis, iPhone cases, wallets, baseball caps, colouring books. His bearded face, akin to someone not making much of an effort when playing Santa Claus, was omnipresent. Colin looked like he was in heaven, as he handed over his credit card to purchase a laptop bag with a cigar smoking Castro emblazoned upon it. The tourist was perhaps unaware of how many orphans and widows Cuba's "Father of the People" created. Apparently, there was a sister store, selling Che Guevara merchandise, in the main terminal of the airport. More than one Marxist had lamentably called Guevara "Christ-like" over the years.

As decided upon beforehand, by the powers that be, the sign read "D A" that the driver, Igor, held up. He stood with a number of other drivers, waiting to collect their prospective passengers, just before the exit to reach the taxi rank. Ambler smiled, pleased to see him. All was going to plan, he thought. *Like clockwork.* The chauffeur was dressed like an undertaker. A leathery, Slavic face, worn away by time and service, peered out beneath a black driver's cap. Sullen or sheepish. Maybe both. Maybe neither. It was difficult to tell.

Through the large glass windows Ambler observed a ragged row of gawping beggars across the street. Some had missing teeth, some had missing limbs. Some waved their hands in front of their faces, either to fan themselves or shoo the flies away. A couple of policemen, carrying well-worn truncheons, flanked them, to prevent the vagrants from accosting the newly arrived tourists.

Before greeting his driver, Ambler also noticed one last advertisement, promoting a neon-lit rooftop bar in the heart of Havana. The venue was called *Revolutionaries*. The image contained a lovestruck couple, more tanned and marketable than Colin and Miranda. The man was kneeling before the enamoured woman, about to propose. The strapline accompanying the ad used a quote from Winston Churchill, of all people:

DUTY CALLS

"Where anything might happen."

23.

Ambler encountered another blast of hair-dryer heat as soon as he stepped out the bounds of the airport. It was a short walk to the car. People were everywhere - black, brown and white faces - speaking a smorgasbord of languages, dressed in all manner of styles, from peasant to princess. Ambler felt like he was drinking the elixir of life, as he poured more cool water down his throat, swishing it around in his mouth beforehand.

Vetrov's driver, Igor, was accompanied by the laconic Dmitri, a security personnel member. Dmitri looked like the boxer Nikolai Valuev's baby, brutal brother. Square head. Six foot something. Big boned. Long-limbed. Dressed in black. Cheap clip-on tie. Sunburnt rather than suntanned. Perspiring. As intimidating as a Varangian. Vetrov must have recently shipped him over, to join his security detail, Ambler fancied. Practical rather than stylish shoes. Comically large earlobes, albeit it was doubtful that anyone dared to crack a joke about them. Humourless rather than garrulous. The Russian nodded and grunted when Igor introduced them.

Ambler's bag was tossed into the boot of the mud-splattered Mercedes with little or no ceremony. The Englishman was instructed to sit in the back. Unfortunately, the air conditioning was as powerful as Bastista in nineteen sixty-one, so the visitor continued to sweat and be sapped by the heat - as sticky as gaffer tape. He would have lazily described it as being "as hot as a furnace" if he were writing a novel. The jabbering radio, which played the Bueno Vista Social Club and gave updates on the weather, drowned out the conspicuous silence between the two Russians in the front. But Ambler was used to Russian staff being surly rather than sociable, especially towards westerners - although they failed to chat to one another as well.

DUTY CALLS

Ambler asked after the health of his host, but he merely received another shrug and grunt from the Lurch-like Russian. The tropical heat was failing to thaw his frosty manner.

The novelist remained content to gaze out of the passenger window, murky with dirt and dead insects, and take in the scenery. They would have to travel though part of Havana to reach the villa. The city was stirring, perhaps waking up from its siesta. People were spilling out into the streets, with cigarettes hanging out of mouths. Plenty of flesh was on show. Too much in some cases, as flab spilled over elasticated waistlines and low-cut tops. There was vibrancy and colour, but also a sense of decay and fading grandeur from its mixed architectural influences, betraying its chequered history. Baroque. Moorish. Modernist. Art Deco. Ambler's head was turned by some of the women, as well as the characterful gas-guzzling old American cars - all wings, grills and fenders - spewing out more smoke than a group of Republican senators at a cigar bar. The one-time historical novelist liked old things. Havana was old. Tired too. A pneumatic drill suddenly went off as they drove along one congested street and Ambler dumbly mistook the sound for a spurt of gunfire for a split second (which was long enough). You could say that now was not the time to be paranoid. But if not now, when? The city was forever just being patched-up rather than re-built in earnest. Parts of Havana looked like parts of Spain in the seventies, with fewer package holidaymakers. The centre of town - with its grand *Capitolio, Plaza de la Catedral and Paseo del Prado* - was impressive and picturesque but swathes of Havana were still mired in privation. Timbers were rotting. Masonry and plaster crumbled off buildings, like a rough sea eating away at a shoreline. The neon and occasional lick of paint was just lipstick on a pig. Hollow expressions were as worn out as the Cuban heels on display. Too many Cuban children were unhealthily skinny and malnourished, as too many American children are obese. Ambler witnessed more than one mange-ridden mongrel, which Sara would have taken pity on and wanted to take home in an instant.

153

Ambler rolled his eyes when he noted another mawkish mural of Fidel and Che on the side of a flaking building. Castro's grip on the country, after the revolution, soon tightened to resemble a fist. Enemies of the state (and allies within his own movement) were disappeared. Where were the murals to thousands of opponents and dissenters who were murdered on Castro's orders? The "Christ-like" Che was fond of summarily executing deserters in the army. The charismatic Castro - as silver-tongued as Mao, as bombastic as Trump and as paranoid as Stalin - understandably spoke more about his universal healthcare system than programme of mass murder. Improved literacy rates after the revolution helped people to swallow his propaganda (as they had little food to eat). Useful idiots sprouted like tobacco. But books were banned as well as read. Businesses (livelihoods) - foreign and domestic - were appropriated by the state. An all-giving but all-consuming government was created. Che Guevara made a better murderer than economist. Not much planning seemed to go into their planned economy. Cuba was a stone's throw away from the US mainland, but a world away in terms of freedom and prosperity. Some Cubans fled after the revolution. Others perished. Plenty turned a blind eye to their deliverer's misdeeds. They still do. Castro knew how to work the press and a photo opportunity, even more than Barack Obama. It seemed that the country was still partly living in the shadow of Castro. Unfortunately. But there was hope, Ambler thought. Reasons to be cheerful. Crucifixes and churches populated the city, as well as iconography concerning Castro and Che. Kind faces outnumbered hollowed out ones. God willing, Catholicism would outlive Communism on the island.

Thinking about politics - and politicians - can be exhausting. The heat was making the author even more world-weary and cynical. Despite the novel scenes around him, Ambler eventually nodded off. When he woke, he found that he had now left the city. The road, as rough as cheap whisky, was now flanked by ramshackle huts as opposed to run-down concrete buildings. Lush farmland could be seen in the distance. The light was fading but it was still hotter than a burlesque show. Ambler would have welcomed some rain, to freshen the muggy air and clean the increased dirt and dead insects off the car.

They began to pass by a few gated villas, similar to the one Vetrov resided in. The properties were probably owned by corrupt government officials or exploitative capitalists. He glimpsed the European cars parked in the driveways. Beautiful wives, or mistresses, doubtless lounged by the pools at the rear of the villas, soaking up the last rays of the sun as they sponged off their spouses.

He would soon reach Vetrov's house. The two men had developed a game of quoting Alexander Pushkin when they met one another. No one can be all that bad if they like Pushkin, the writer thought. Usually, the stout Russian would let out a roar and give his English friend a bear hug and clap him on the back three times when they met. Such was the Russian's health, however, that Ambler tempered any expectations.

Even more than Vetrov though, or Maria, Ambler started to picture in his mind's eye the two agents who were due to meet him outside the *Hotel Inglaterra*. They would be working in shifts, waiting for the joe to arrive to handover the flash drive. The treasure. One of them would casually walk by and ask their fellow Englishman for a light. Ambler would oblige and give the agent the drive, as well as a brass *Zippo* lighter he had dug out from a drawer in his flat for the occasion. After the handoff he would then be free. Happy. Honour fulfilled. Duty couldn't ask any more of him for a few months, at least.

The gates to the villa creaked open. Despite his nap in the car Ambler still felt uncommonly drained – and he hadn't even done anything remarkable or heroic yet. For some time now he had felt like life, or death, was catching up with him. Or perhaps he was just being a conceited novelist.

He got out of the car and surveyed the property. Splashes of piss-like sunlight poured through the overhanging trees. The yellow plasterwork appeared more jaundiced than in the photographs he had seen. Tiles were missing from the roof. The guttering needed clearing and weeds outnumbered flowers in the garden. The oligarch had fallen from grace.

Igor retrieved the Englishman's bag.

"Will you also be driving me back?" Ambler asked.

The Russian remained mute, but his expression suggested that the answer was "no".

As Ambler walked up the drive, its flagstones worn and cracked, his lower back began to throb, flare-up, like it was trying to tell him something. Warn him.

24.

"He's here," Yuri remarked, with no discernible emotion, as he entered the reception room at the rear of the villa. The bodyguard then took out his pistol and chambered a round. It was unlikely that the novelist would resist, or attempt anything out of the ordinary, but the Russian prided himself on being a professional. One should plan for any and all circumstances.

His employer pursed his lips. He told himself to remain calm. He had been waiting for what seemed like an age for this moment. He breathed heavily. Snorted. One hand balled itself into a fist, the other cradled a whisky tumbler, filled with vodka, ice and a slice of lemon. The Russian had envisioned this scene more than once, during the past month or so. In several of the scenarios he had just pictured himself pulling out a gun and emptying it into the Englishman. Without a word said, consumed by rage and revenge. But he was a businessman, not a barbarian. He needed the author to know what he was being punished for. Without self-control, it is difficult to control anything else. He checked his watch. Tapped it. Twice. The author was on time. He would not be late for his own funeral, as the saying went.

Igor opened the front door for the guest, bowed his head and then retreated to the car. His instructions were to drive home. Dmitri remained behind Ambler, ushering him forward. Ambler headed down the hallway, towards the reception room, his footsteps sounding on the parquet flooring. He saw a couple of people, who he didn't recognise, waiting for him. He walked past a flight of stairs to his right. On his left, hanging on the wall, was a painting of the Battle of Borodino. A black and white photo of a trio of soldiers in the Red Army (Vetrov believed the image included an antecedent of his) hung next to the specially commissioned artwork.

The large, glass doors at the back of the reception room looked out onto the swimming pool and a dull, orange sky. They were open. Warm air oozed through them. A couple of Russian icons, of Christ and Mary, in the early Byzantine style, decorated the wall to Ambler's left, as he entered the room. They hung over an antique rosewood table, with brass or gold feet, which housed an antique, silver samovar set. In the far corner was a previously well-stocked bar. Several varnished oak bookcases lined the room. Should Ambler have had the time and will to investigate them more, he would have discovered a few of his own titles in his host's library. In the centre of the room was a L-shaped sofa - expensive but tired looking. There were a few stains on the piece of furniture, from where the infirm owner had spilled coffee or relieved himself. The sofa faced a sixty inch plus flatscreen TV, which was showing a Brazilian football match on mute. *Corinthians* were playing *Santos*. The former were four goals up and there were only ten minutes remaining.

Tucked away in the corner by the television, near the entrance to the kitchen, sat a barely recognisable Yevgeny Vetrov. Wheelchair bound. Quite literally half the man he used to be, given the weight he had lost. A few strands of lank hair hung down from his liver-spotted scalp. Horrifically gaunt. As jaundiced as the walls outside. He had been dressed in a medical gown, which failed to cover-up his skinny, varicose-veined legs. He was close to death, Ambler suspected. It was surprising that flies were not congregating over his head, in anticipation of feasting on a corpse. The debilitated Vetrov reminded Ambler of his own father, when the doctor advised that they could only now offer the patient palliative care. Cancer had eaten away at the Russian, on the outside and in. An oxygen mask covered his mouth. The wheelchair was electric, but it appeared that its user neither had the strength or wherewithal to steer it. Ambler couldn't be sure if he noticed a flicker of recognition, as Vetrov turned his head towards the new person who had entered the room. Perhaps he did. His eyes were both piteous and pitiful. Ambler's heart went out to the Russian, but he was understandably more concerned for his own welfare.

The smartly dressed figure (wearing a linen suit which made Ambler's now creased effort appear pauper-esque) standing in front of the joe possessed the same iron-grey hair and beak of a nose as Viktor Rybin, but the resemblance ended there. Birch had remarked that Rybin looked like the lovechild of Molotov, Himmler and Goebbels. "Not the most pleasant threesome one would like to imagine," Ambler retorted, with a pinched expression. The well-built figure in front of him, despite his pensionable age, appeared as if he might have been sired by Zhukov or Heydrich. Piercing blue eyes. Chiselled jawline. Capped teeth. His pungent, but manly, cologne filled the air. His unblinking gaze was intense, as if he were trying to bore - or burn - his way into Ambler's soul.

"You do not know me. But I know you. You are the man responsible for the death of my son in a car accident, earlier in the year. My name is Oleg Volkov. My son's name was Alyosha. After the accident he checked himself out of the hospital and went to Paris, the following day, where he met his mother. That evening he collapsed in his hotel room, as a result of a concussion, and fell into a coma. I arranged for him to be taken care of at a special clinic in Zurich. I sat by his bedside each day. I prayed, each night, in the chapel there. My son never regained consciousness. He passed away just over a month ago. I did not get to say goodbye or tell him how much I love him. Parents should not outlive their children. But I did promise my son that I would find and punish the man responsible for his death. My son was no innocent, but he did not deserve to have his life cut short. I tried to protect him from this world, from my world. But it turned out that I could not protect him from you."

Ambler's mind raced around, like a hamster on a wheel, trying to keep up and comprehend what was unfolding. He had heard the name Oleg Volkov before. The Russian was an industrialist. A shipping magnate. He was known for opening-up ports, all around Europe and Asia, to crime syndicates - providing legal cover for them and laundering their ill-gotten gains. He was a former KGB officer. Like many senior figures in the Russian intelligence service, Volkov turned the fall of the Soviet Union into an opportunity. A business opportunity, to seize money and power.

159

Volkov was tasked by the Communist Party to find missing state funds, funds which Volkov himself and his friends had embezzled. The KGB officer was a man who was not afraid to get his hands dirty, or bloody. Using his connections in the intelligence community, the military and with the Bratva, the once devout communist became a convert to capitalism, intent on protecting and expending his empire. The enemy had once been American imperialism. Now the enemy was anything which prevented him from making more money. Competitors were liquidated. Government officials were bribed or threatened. Former soldiers and KGB operatives were put on the payroll. The businessman rewarded success and punished failure, in relation to his employees and associates. The Russian travelled extensively and enjoyed the finer things in life. But business always came before pleasure. He married his secretary, Arina. He knew that, whether out of fear or loyalty, she would never betray him. Arina was also wise enough to turn a blind eye to her husband's affairs with subsequent secretaries and mistresses. Arina was devoted to her son. She lived for him. Spoiled him. Called him every day. Oversaw his education. Frightened off any whores or gold diggers who tried to take advantage of her sweet boy. After a short period of mourning, Arina encouraged her husband to "find him" - which Volkov duly interpreted as "kill him". But the vengeful Russian had already sentenced the Englishman to death by that point. Killing the author would not entirely assuage his grief, but it would help. Grief was eating away at the sonless father like cancer had eaten away at Vetrov. He believed that he would feel better once he had dealt with the Englishman. The scales of justice would not seem so out of kilter. He could be at peace. Sleep at night. A line would be drawn under events and the Russian could get back to business.

Ambler was briefly tempted to protest that the man's son had crashed into him and been responsible for his own death, but he felt it imprudent to interrupt the Russian. Oligarchs didn't take too kindly to being contradicted. The author also needed to still process what was happening. The realisation dawned upon him, sending a chill down his perspiring spine, that Ambler could be even closer to death than the poor soul sitting in the corner.

"You were fortunate, initially, in that I was not granted permission to travel to London to carry out what I needed to do. The powers that be wanted to cool their activities in the capital. There was also the danger of being apprehended or caught on camera in London. It would be bad for business. But I am not a man to be easily deterred. Moscow would permit the hit, just not in Britain. I had a former colleague put together a file on you, to ascertain any weak spots you might have. I noted your connection with Yevgeny. Dmitri, would you take our host back to his room? He is not the most pleasant sight to look at and his heart might not be able to take what comes next," Volkov remarked, matter-of-factly. Dmitri duly marched over to the withered figure and wheeled him to his bedroom. Aside from Igor, Vetrov's staff, including his nurse, had been instructed to take the day off. "I had dealings with Yevgeny. He was a force to be reckoned with, back in his day. Now he could be considered collateral damage in the operation I had in mind. He may not be long for this earth, but he has a son and daughter. Do not blame him for wanting to sacrifice his friend, to protect his family. During my time in the service - and in business - I have had cause to flush people out of hiding. I just needed to find what type of cheese I needed to dangle over the rat hole, to lure you out. I had to plot as hard as any novelist, you might say. Usually, one would just offer the promise of money to entice one's prey to come out of their burrow. But, rightly or wrongly, I thought I needed to incentivise you in another way. I would promise you the prize of redemption or a good conscience. I should say that the cost of this operation is greater than any mere cash sum I would have offered. I had to pay a significant amount to a trusted asset of your service, to act as an intermediary, supposedly representing Yevgeny, when selling the operation to MI6. He has been suitably compensated for any loss of earnings from the British that he might now suffer. I knew that your Boyd Hamilton would believe what he wanted to believe. One need only plant a seed in a man's mind. Vanity and ambition will compel it to grow. I have encountered his type before. A peacock, feathering his nest. Your politicians and civil servants deserve each other. At the KGB, we would have thought the offer to be too good to be true. I was also confident that Hamilton would want to hoard all the glory and not involve the Americans. And so you fell for the ruse - hook, line and sinker."

Volkov finally stopped talking. The short silence was broken by the noise of Yuri cracking his knuckles. The bodyguard's eyes naturally flitted around the room, as restless as a sparrow hopping from branch to branch. His back faced towards the glass doors. Ideally, he should have positioned himself to take in both main entrances into the room (although he had posted one of his men out by the pool). He was keen to observe the exchange between his boss and the Englishman. Yuri was still unsure as to how long he would need to torture his victim for, before killing him. The former FSB officer had laid out various instruments on a drinks trolley down in the cellar. A hammer. Pliers. Plastic bag. Acid. A drill. He had also furnished the chamber with medical provisions, to revive the Englishman should his paymaster wish to prolong the Englishman's torment. Personally, Yuri was keen for it to be all over as quickly as possible. He wanted to get back to the security and comfort of their base of operations in Geneva. The stinging heat, insects and feckless inhabitants of the island didn't agree with the Muscovite.

The quiet was also shattered by the sound of the third and final member of Volkov's security detail suddenly slapping his neck, as he killed a mosquito. Gennady was notably younger than his two colleagues. His attention was often more focused on the football match than the scene being played out in front of him. Gennady had peroxide-blond hair and a tan, gleaned from trips to the solarium in Geneva rather than his short stay in Havana. His face was a picture of scorn, as if he were looking at a Chechen rebel, as he inspected the remnants of the dead insect on his palm.

Ambler finally spoke. Half-choked, as if an invisible hand were clasped around his throat.

"It was an accident. Your son drove into me."

DUTY CALLS

"I have not brought you here to have you protest your innocence," Volkov remarked with a sneer, his voice momentarily increasing in volume, like he had been insulted. "What's done is done. My son could not be saved. Nor can you be saved. Your intelligence service will call what happens here "an accident". They will be keen to forget the embarrassment. Your name will be swept under the carpet. They will not want to be reminded of their failure. I come from their world. I know how they think."

Yuri pulled out his gun. He hoped that the action might prompt his employer to end the conversation - and for them to all go downstairs.

The sky now appeared to be a grey brown. Sludge. A stain on the world. The light was fading - and a pall was falling over Ambler's inward eye. His mouth was as dry as a Jewish sense of humour. He felt sick, nauseated - a world away from redemption and a good conscience. Perhaps he was now paying for his sins. It was difficult to know how close the author was to begging for his life. It wasn't due to pride that he didn't do so, but more the social awkwardness - and futility - of the gesture. He inwardly cursed his old friend. Birch had manipulated him, after being manipulated himself. At best he was incompetent, at worst perfidious. Spying is misdirection. Spying is disinformation. The professionals should know this. The promise of treasure had burned so brightly that it had blinded them. Ambler also cursed himself for falling - or leaping - into the trap. A novelist is supposed to possess some form of insight. As angry as he was, Ambler also felt other stages of grief in rapid succession (there was seemingly little time left and who else would grieve for him?) - depression and bargaining. If he could be granted a last request, aside from his life being spared, he wanted the chance to compose another message to Sara and send it. Perhaps Ambler negotiated various stages of grief because, for a long time, he had accepted his fate. Maybe the Catholic wanted something to die for, rather than live for. The first passage from Shakespeare which the

163

teenage Ambler ever memorised was from *Measure For Measure*:

"Be absolute for death…"

Operation Pancho Villa may be life in microcosm. Well-intended but ill-judged. A betrayal. Sham. A joke, with an unfunny punchline.

The TV flashed. Another goal had been scored. *Corinthians* were five nil up. Surely it was even more of a lost cause for *Santos* now? Their fate was sealed.

Ambler's heart had galloped, from fear and anxiety. But it now slowed. Fatigued. Close to stopping. His race was run - and Ambler was too weary to care about whether he had come first or last. There were worse fates than oblivion.

Volkov lifted his glass up and took a sip of vodka. He winced slightly, experiencing another pang of grief, recalling how his son would also often order the same drink. It was time to torture and kill the Englishman.

25.

Yuri Tasarov didn't quite think of any and all circumstances in relation to protecting his client, but there was no time for regret as the left side of his skull exploded from a suppressed round, turning his head inside out - like a piece of popcorn.

The sound of a silenced pistol is far louder than most people imagine. Far louder than the movies. Everyone in the room started, aside from the man who fired the gun. James Marshal.

Oliver Porter had arranged the weapon. Marshal picked it up from the fixer's contact in Havana, shortly after he landed that morning. The cash in the envelope which Ambler passed to him, in the *American Bar*, more than covered the cost of the used *Browning Hi-Power* pistol. Before handing him the money that afternoon Ambler had spoken about what had unfolded that week, from his lunch in the *Skylon* to his final debrief concerning *Operation Pancho Villa*. The new recruit had broken the Official Secrets Act (it was not the first or last time for a spy to do so). Spying is duplicity. Ambler was keen for the private sector to cover any deficiencies in the public sector. More than one spook over the years had told him to trust no one. But he could trust Marshal. The soldier, as opposed to spy, still possessed a vestige of honour.

"You don't need to do this, of course," Ambler remarked, jittery from the gravitas of the operation, the gravity of committing treason and putting his friend in such an awkward position. He was also uncomfortable and unused to asking for favours. "I'd just feel better if someone had my back."

"I know I don't need to. I don't even want to. But I'll be there," Marshal replied, reassuringly, as he already began to think how he would need to contact Oliver Porter. He would feel a lot more confident watching over his friend and client with a weapon in his hands. Happiness is a warm gun.

After collecting the pistol and a clunker of a car from Miguel (the former PMC had met shadier characters in his profession before, just not not many; thankfully he trusted Porter enough to trust his Cuban associate), Marshal drove towards Vetrov's villa, parking the vehicle a quarter of a mile away from the property. He reconnoitred the location (keeping a note of the number of potential hostiles), having bought a pair of binoculars at an inflated price from Miguel. Marshal joked to himself that the Cuban had seen him coming.

He waited. Soldiering is waiting. Marshal posted himself in some at the rear of the villa, just behind the wall, with a good view of the pool area and reception room. From his vantage point in the woods Marshal observed the car drive through the gates. Ambler got out. It was when he witnessed one of the Russians chamber a round that the soldier was triggered. The hairs went up on the back of his sunburnt neck. Something was amiss. Marshal stealthily climbed over the wall and moved closer to the house, easily avoiding the attention of the sentry who was conveniently facing the opposite way. Having fired a suppressed gun more than once he knew that he would lose any element of surprise if he shot the guard by the pool house, so he rendered him unconscious with a choke hold and moved the body out of sight.

When he spied the Russian pulling out his gun, Marshal knew that it was time to use his. He gave his word to Ambler that he would have his back. Duty called. The soldier turned his moral switch on, or off, depending on one's viewpoint.

If his one-man ambush was going to work, it needed to work quickly. Marshal was the only figure in the room whose attention wasn't drawn to the sight of the half-headless Russian. He was too busy lining up his next target.

The next bullet ripped through Oleg Volkov's body and shattered the glass tumbler he was holding. Or rather two bullets punched their way through his spine and sternum. Two shots, in quick succession - like when the shipping magnate tapped his watch. Volkov's usually stony expression was briefly contorted in utter shock or utter agony.

Ambler was understandably surprised to see the gunman appear through the door, albeit less surprised than others and in a different way. A good way. The soldier was the soul of focus and precision. Murder on his mind. An alloy of training and experience. Dressed in a dark, lightweight jacket, russet t-shirt, bark-brown chinos and black trainers. The gun a natural extension of his body.

The smell of cordite already began to oust Volkov's cologne. It was a gunfight. The reception room could have been a cantina in New Mexico. Marshal could have been John Wesley Hardin. There was the quick and the dead during such encounters. Gennady fell next, swatted like an insect, as his hand fished limply and lamely for the pistol contained in his shoulder holster beneath his suit jacket. Again, two shots. The first bullet took a bite-sized chunk from out of the young man's neck, the second caused his heart to burst like a balloon. Beneath his tan the enforcer started to turn deathly pale. Streaks of blood marked the piss-soaked sofa and the Russian's blond hair.

Dmitri had heard the sound of gunfire, suppressed or otherwise, before. He had been shot before - and he had fired his own weapon and killed before. The large Russian (when Marshal saw him earlier, he thought he resembled Richard Kiel) didn't panic. Out of the corner of his eye Ambler saw Dmitri retrieve his large *Magnum Desert Eagle* pistol, recently cleaned and oiled, whilst he swore in Russian.

Dmitri was quick. But Marshal was quicker.

But it was the Englishman's turn to swear as his pistol jammed. The gun was now as useful as a senior civil servant.

The Russian continued to swear, yet on observing how helpless his opponent was his face broke into a lop-sided grin, revealing a set of large, off-white teeth - lined up like a row of gravestones. He even smiled like Richard Kiel. Marshal was now target practice - and the Russian wouldn't miss from such close range. Dmitri wrapped his two gigantic hands around the pistol and raised his arms, his suit stretching across his broad shoulders.

167

It was instinctual. Rage and something else compelled Ambler to act - without him altogether thinking about it - to try and save the man who had tried to save him. The author, who was more accustomed to literary spats, launched himself at the hulking bodyguard. With more strength and courage than he would have given himself credit for, Ambler succeeded in disturbing Dmitri's aim. The shot went over Marshal's head and created a fist-like hole in the stucco ceiling. Ambler did his best to grapple with the Russian and disarm him - but size matters. The fearsome professional soon shook off his assailant and shoved him to the ground, accompanied by some now ubiquitous curses. Ambler emitted a species of yowl as he landed on his arse and jarred his injured coccyx one more time. Despite the spike in his adrenalin, he remained on the floor. Defeated.

Ambler stared up at the grim Russian. His willing executioner. The darkness had swelled even more. The gun loomed just as large as its handler. He was just now waiting for the muzzle flash, like a dragon spitting fire, and then there would likely be complete darkness. There are no happy endings. Turgenev would have agreed. Ambler closed his eyes. Resigned to his fate. Almost at peace. Or praying.

Two shots rang out.

Ambler's prayers were answered. He opened his eyes to observe the Russian staggering backwards, collapsing against a bookcase. Gut shot. Marshal hadn't hesitated. He had dropped the *Browning Hi-Power* and raced towards the *Glock* on the floor next to Yuri's corpse, whilst Ambler kept the bodyguard occupied. A round had already been chambered. Ready and waiting.

Another two shots shattered the balmy air, thudding into Dmitri's chest. Like nails being hammered into a coffin. Bloodstains bloomed like roses across the slab of his torso.

It was over. Even Marshal was sweating and appeared perturbed. But not for long.

"I'm not sure whether trouble sometimes finds me, or I find trouble," he remarked, a little breathlessly.

168

Ambler was still somewhat in shock. Things were a blur, and he couldn't quite tell if his friend was being rueful or joking. It was becoming more apparent to the author that Marshal could be considered a sociopath, thank God. A well-adjusted human being, whatever that was, would have never got on the plane to Cuba and gunned down four people.

Marshal proceeded to wipe his prints from the two guns - and place them in the palms of Volkov and his bodyguard. Vetrov, still ensconced in his bedroom, could not be judged a reliable witness. The ailing Russian wasn't quite as dead as the men splayed around his living room, but he wasn't far off. Hopefully the police would tie things up in a bow for themselves and conclude that the visitors had gunned down each other.

"What do we do now?" Ambler asked, still only half in possession of his faculties.

"We get the heck out of Dodge," Marshal replied.

Volkov's countenance still seemed to offer up an accusatory expression as Ambler walked past the corpse, careful of avoiding the burgeoning pool of blood, as he took his leave. It had just started with a prang, on a dull night in Earl's Court, a few months ago. And it had ended up here, like this. The shock of it all would remain in his blood, malaria-like, for years to come.

The two men made their way under the cover of darkness, accompanied by a chorus of crickets. The air was fragrant with the scent of flowers (heliconia and yellow bells). Ambler's legs buckled beneath him a couple of times, but Marshal encouraged and supported his companion. The heat and near-death experience had exhausted him. He resembled a drunk, in some respects. Ironically, the author hadn't touched a drop all day, for once.

They reached the mud-brown old Ford, as rundown as Ambler. The plan was to drive to the airport and take the first flight to the US or Europe. It would be a long night's journey into day.

"Put your seatbelt on," Marshal told his passenger, who still didn't seem fully compos mentis. He looked haunted. "We don't want to have an accident."

"No, we don't," Ambler replied, after a pause, not quite knowing how comic or tragic the statement was. It was probably both.

26. Epilogue.

Ambler was blessed with falling into a restorative sleep during the flight back from Boston to Heathrow. Once he landed, the recruit called his handler. He would have done so sooner, but he wanted to make Birch sweat. Punish him a little.

"Do you have the file?" Birch asked, with more than a hint of desperation - without first enquiring after his joe's welfare.

"There was no file. Just a fuck-up," Ambler replied, with more than a hint of curtness. He then demanded an immediate meet.

Ambler and Marshal went their separate ways at the airport. The author, who usually frowned upon displays of public affection or emotion, hugged and thanked his friend once more.

"Barring charges of treason, I'll be in touch in a day or so," Ambler half-joked.

He may have broken the protocol of being a spy, but Ambler decided that honesty would be the best policy when recounting events to Birch (Tanner and Palmer were also present at the house in Knightsbridge; the latter sat with a pen and legal pad in front of him). The novelist did not have the energy to make anything up.

Ambler spoke about the car accident, employing Marshal and the events at the villa (he chose to leave out his encounter with Connor Mason, though, deeming it irrelevant or embarrassing). The three men took in the report, enthralled - and ashamed. There had been a blatant failure of intelligence on the service's part - and they had dispatched an innocent civilian to be tortured and executed. Not their finest hour.

"We should call this Marshal in to make him sign a section -"

"We should call him in to give him a commendation, for pulling our arses out of the fire," Tanner said, cutting Palmer off. If looks could kill, Palmer would have been dead. The soldier had done his job over in Cuba. If only the spies had done theirs, he judged.

As Ambler suspected, there would be a détente of mutually assured destruction concerning the operation. The joe would not prosecute the service, for fear of being punished over breaking the Official Secrets Act. Conversely, the service would not punish their errant operative for fear of advertising their incompetence and opening themselves up to being sued.

"Least said, soonest mended," Birch remarked, before forcing an emollient smile.

Spying is remembering to forget.

Ambler couldn't muster the requisite politeness to smile back. He just wanted to go home, to a glass of whisky and a good book - kick the dust off his feet from the whole affair. A spy's life was not for him. Being a spy novelist was exciting enough. The world could save itself.

Boyd Hamilton ensured that *Operation Pancho Villa* would not become even a codicil upon a footnote in the annals of the service's history. It was important that both the press - and his equally ambitious rivals in the service - remained in the dark. He even cancelled a weekend away with his mistress to keep on top of things. "To put out a fire before it starts."

Scapegoating and passing the buck were tantamount to Victorian parlour games at the River House, perhaps having adopted a certain culture from their colleagues in Whitehall. In the blink of an eye Boyd Hamilton knew where to assign blame.

"You and your team must take ownership of any errors in judgement, Simon. Root out those who are culpable. Transfer them if need be. DFID is always in need of over-keen idiots… You must know that you have blotted your own copybook too. But if you learn from your mistakes then perhaps this farrago may not prove such a complete waste of time… We need to deal with our intermediary too. The asset has become a liability. Burn him."

Birch decided to take his medicine, noting how Hamilton had called the asset "his" intermediary before the operation had turned into their very own Bay of Pigs.

As a further punishment Hamilton ordered his subordinate to personally "check and re-check the bona fides" of their other relevant assets. "We cannot afford for this to happen again on your watch," he pointedly remarked. Such was the weight of work now on his desk that he would have few windows to meet his girlfriends. Birch sighed, or even harrumphed, thinking how he would have to spend more time with his wife and family at home.

Later that day the two men met again, to discuss a communique from their US counterparts. They flagged up intelligence of increased Russian army activity on the Ukrainian border. They also asked for any intelligence they had on one Viktor Rybin. The US were raising the threat level for a military incursion. Boyd Hamilton remained unfazed, however, believing that their American cousins were just getting over-excited again.

"My nose tells me that it is just Russian posturing."

"I agree," Birch replied, although he might have uttered those two words regardless of anything his boss said.

Events were still raw and understandably uncomfortable for Ambler to embark upon writing another spy novel, set in Cuba or elsewhere. Instead, he started work on a proposal for a biography of Turgenev. The working title was *An Unrequited Life*. As melancholy as they might make him feel, Ambler was looking forward to reading his subject's novels again. He would likely suffer a small loss in income, but he was hopeful of making gains in other areas.

After a couple of days of working, drinking and sleeping Ambler called his ex-wife. He couldn't think of a pretext to see her - or he didn't want to lie to her - so he just asked if she was free to meet. He just wanted to be in her company, even if just as a friend. Second best was good enough.

"Can I see you later?"

"I'm going to mass."

"Do you mind if I come along too?"

"No, of course not."

It seemed strange, or sacred, crossing the threshold of the church. He genuflected with genuine reverence. He breathed in the smell of the candles like perfume, in the same way that Marshal probably breathed in the smell of cordite. The priest was sanctimonious and far too progressive - and the sermon bored him - but Ambler enjoyed the poetry and potency of the hymns.

"Beloved Father, hear my lamentations,
Timely is the cry of woe of this miserable wretch.
O heart of my heart, whatever befall me,
O ruler of all, be thou my vision."

There was a moment when Ambler retreated into himself and he appeared haunted once more, but Sara gently squeezed his hand and brought him back to the land of the living. A couple of members of *The Blackheath Writing Society* were in attendance too, and they made a beeline for the novelist after the service. Before they could bombard him with questions or requests, though, Sara saved him by saying they had to leave as they were late for their lunch date.

Was he now an un-lapsed Catholic? The writer realised that it was deeds, rather than words, which mattered. It was perhaps worth declaring himself a Catholic just to shock or offend the gaggle of atheists and liberals in his circle.

Before leaving the church, Ambler was mindful of lighting a candle and saying a prayer for Alyosha Volkov. The Catholic wasn't sufficiently Christian to spare a prayer for Oleg Volkov, needless to say.

Marshal proposed to Grace. When she asked him about when he decided that he wanted to marry her, Marshal failed to mention that it was at the moment a Russian goon pointed a *Magnum Desert Eagle* pistol at his person. If he was going to be a good husband, it was best he learned how to be a convincing liar - sooner rather than later. Sometimes there are happy-*ish* endings.

End Note.

More than one reader asked, after finishing a draft of the manuscript, if *Duty Calls* is based on a true story. The answer is no - and please don't take denial to mean confirmation in this instance. One reader also commented that I had sailed close to the wind and perhaps been too accurate when pulling back the curtain in relation to the publishing world and the life of an author. Please know that my intention is to always first amuse rather than offend, although I must confess that I don't much care if some people get offended. Duty calls.

I have namechecked more than one spy novelist in the text who I would recommend you read, if you have not done so already. Should you be interested in some background reading about Putin's Russia then you should check out *From Russia With Blood* by Heidi Blake and *Putin's People* by Catherine Belton.

I can also recommend that you listen to the songs mentioned throughout the book, as a soundtrack whilst you're reading.

Although the novel is the first in a series to feature Daniel Ambler, for those of you interested in the character of James Marshal, he is the protagonist in the thrillers *Enough Is Enough* and *Blood For Blood*. Oliver Porter features in those books, as well as in the Michael Devlin series of novellas *Nothing To Lose*, *Darkness Visible* and *Ready For Anything*.

Please feel free to get in touch should you have enjoyed any of the novels. I can be contacted via richard@sharpebooks.com

Thomas Waugh.

Printed in Great Britain
by Amazon